GROUSE HUNTING STRATEGIES

Books by Frank Woolner

GROUSE AND GROUSE HUNTING

SPEARHEAD IN THE WEST

THE COMPLETE BOOK OF STRIPED BASS FISHING
(with Henry Lyman)

THE COMPLETE BOOK OF WEAKFISHING
(with Henry Lyman)

THE SPORTSMAN'S COMPANION
(with Henry Lyman, E. C. Janes, and Clyde Ormond)

GROUSE HUNTING STRATEGIES

A Handbook of Hunting Techniques

Frank Woolner

Foreword by
William G. Tapply

THE LYONS PRESS

ACKNOWLEDGMENTS

SPECIAL THANKS are due to Horace G. Tapply, Henry Lyman, E. Michael "Bill" Pollack, Paul Kukonen, and my brothers, Jack and Dick Woolner, all of whom read the first draft of this manuscript and offered constructive criticism.

I am further indebted to the following valued contributors of specialized information and photographs: Dr. Sanford W. Schemnitz, Jack Swedberg, and Carl Scott, Charles F. Waterman, Bob Elliot, Erwin A. Bauer, and Leonard Lee Rue III.

Ivon Keller Woolner, my sister-in-law, was kind enough to type the final draft while I engaged in some inescapable business like striped bass fishing or deer hunting. (Upland shooting was not then in season.)

10 9 8 7 6 5 4 3 2 1

Printed in Canada

The Library of Congress Cataloging-in-Publication Data is available on file.

CONTENTS

FOREWORD

Among shotgunners who have made their acquaintance, ruffed grouse consistently arouse the strongest passions. All agree that the partridge is the smartest, wildest, hardest-flying, and altogether most challenging, frustrating, and lovable game bird on two wings.

Such a bird deserves a passionate chronicler, and no man I've known or whose stories I've read was more passionate—about life, about writing, about friends, about hunting and fishing, about the outdoors in general, and about ruffed grouse in particular—than Frank Woolner.

"Mine is a love story," he writes, "a sometimes personal treatise on the game bird that is more important to me than wild geese coursing an autumn sky, than black ducks cupping their wings and dropping into the blocks, than woodcock spiraling over the alders in the red hush of an October twilight."

Like so many outdoor writers of his generation, Frank Woolner was a generalist, a jack of all trades and a master of most of them. He spent his life in the New England out-of-doors, passionately devouring whatever the season offered. He hunted upland birds and waterfowl, rabbits and squirrels, foxes and deer. He cast flies and drifted worms for brook trout, and he heaved live eels and wooden plugs into the Cape Cod surf for striped bass. When no game or fish was in season, he tromped the fields and forests anyway, absorbing nature's stories.

And he wrote with absolute authority about all of it. He's probably best known for his fanatical devotion to surf casting—he wrote several books and countless articles on the subject, and he edited *Salt Water Sportsman* for more than thirty years. But do not doubt that he was equally an authority on ruffed grouse.

I grew up believing that men like Frank Woolner had the best job imaginable. He stocked his memory cupboard by fishing and hunting, and he called it research. He went out and had adventures, and then he wrote about them—and people gave him money for it. What a life!

He was a storyteller, deft with dialogue, pitch-perfect in rhythm and mood, quick with the apt figure of speech, tuned into all five of the senses. You didn't need to know—or care—about hunting and fishing to lose yourself in his words. Listen to the man: "There is something indescribably delicious about clean swamp mud and the pungent perfume of a working farm, things soul-satisfying in birdsong and frogs chunking and bees sampling a field of clover. There is cold magic in an ice storm and the deep, soft drift of snow stitched with the elfin tracks of field mice."

Back in the thirties and forties, my father edited a sporting magazine called *Hunting and Fishing*. Dad bought Frank Woolner's first outdoor story and thereby helped to launch a career that lasted half a century.

Dad launched a lot of other careers, too, and being the man he was (and still is), he often ended up hunting and fishing with the writers he did business with. I was the lucky kid who got to tag along. Thus I made the acquaintance of a whole generation of sporting writers, including the man who signed his letters "Von Woolner."

Frank Woolner shared the tangled grouse covert behind his house in Shrewsbury, Massachusetts, with me. Later, when I aspired to emulate his lifestyle that I so envied, he also shared his wisdom on the writing business with me, as he did unselfishly with countless other novice outdoor writers. He taught me that it wasn't as easy as it looked, and he encouraged me when I needed encouragement. "Unlike some editors," recalled Hal Lyman, Frank's lifelong friend, co-editor, and collaborator on several saltwater fishing books, "he would go out of his way to encourage a young new writer in whose work he saw a spark of potential to improve and develop his theme. At times, a two-page letter of encouragement took the place of a stark rejection slip."

Frank Woolner learned to write the same way he learned to catch stripers and hunt grouse—by trying and erring and pondering it and trying some more. He had a high-school education, but he was a voracious and wide-ranging reader. "Many who met him in the field," Lyman wrote, "were startled when this tough outdoorsman quoted poetry—ranging from Kipling to Frost—at length."

I'm not sure how many stories Frank ended up selling after that first one that my father bought. Several hundred, certainly. Besides his duties at *Salt Water Sportsman*, he published about a dozen books, including this one and *The Complete Book of Woodcock Hunting*, its companion piece on woodcock, both of which are classics.

He wrote about hunting and fishing, yes. But he also wrote about the chill of an autumn afternoon and the warmth of the sun's rays when they reflect off a pewter sea. For many years his wide-ranging outdoors columns appeared in the Worcester (Massachusetts) *Sunday Telegram*, the best of which he collected in 1972 in an anthology called *My New England*. He wrote about robins and bats, wildflowers and stone walls, mosquitoes and tree frogs—which Frank called, delightfully and evocatively, "the bells of springtime."

When Frank Woolner died in 1994, he was still counseling young writers, turning out silky prose on all manner of outdoorsy subjects, and sharing his hard-earned wisdom on the comings and goings of striped bass, bluefish, flounder, and weakfish for *Salt Water Sportsman*. And that, I've learned, is how outdoor writers do it. They hunt and they fish, and they wander around in the woods, and they write until they drop. They never really retire from doing what's in their blood.

What a life!

Frank Woolner began writing in a simpler time, when the morality of the "blood sports" was rarely challenged by animal rights activists or anti-gun crusaders. A thoughtful man, however, didn't need a challenge to think about it. "I make no apology for being a gunner and an angler," he wrote, "but I am a hunter without malice and maybe a fisher who seeks much more than any limit catch of trout."

Today's naturalists might raise an eyebrow at Frank's readiness to shoot grouse predators, but his reasoning was neither simplistic nor hard-headed. Nobody understood the complexities of nature's ways better than Frank Woolner. "It is characteristic of well-meaning yet ill-informed nature lovers to insist that all predators are beneficial," he wrote. "This product of wishful thinking contains just enough truth to make it dangerous."

On the other hand, he understood that "extremists who rant that every flesh-eating bird or mammal should be shot on sight betray an abject ignorance of wildlife dynamics."

Woolner's middle ground is based on a commonsense understanding of nature's interconnectedness, coupled with his unabashed love for ruffed grouse. "If I am hunting in a state where the great horned owl is unprotected," he declared, "I will shoot each and every one that shows in upland cover. . . . I have a bone to pick with do-gooders who have convinced legislatures that the great horned owl should be protected at all seasons. Ill-informed nature lovers are robbing Peter to pay Paul: the ruffed grouse suffers."

Grouse Hunting Strategies contains equal parts of natural history and hunting lore. The book is proof that the love of nature and the love of hunting go hand-in-hand. As much as he cherished grouse, I can vouch for the fact that Frank hunted them hard and never lost track of the point of it. He liked to find birds, and he liked to shoot them, and he was very good at both. His lifetime of accumulated grouse-hunting wisdom is contained in these pages. The chapters on recognizing likely grouse cover, wingshooting, hunting with and without dogs, and choosing guns and other gear remain as fresh and practical as they were thirty years ago when he wrote them.

Grouse hunting is hard work. Frank liked that. It's what made it worthwhile. "You will hike the birch woods and struggle through junipers and bullbrier, breast laurel jungles, and scrub oak thickets. You will pause to take a breather after steaming climbs to beech ridges and plateaus where mountain winds are keen in the pines and hemlocks. If you decide to hunt partridges, one thing is certain: you'll walk."

But "every grouse hunter is an incurable romantic, else he would not seek this bird above all others," and Frank Woolner was surely a romantic. "Usually," he wrote, "during the final afternoon of a grouse-hunting season, I take pleasure in tracking a fast-flying pat with my shotgun and, instead of pressing the trigger, I grin crookedly and lower the piece. There is a secret satisfaction in this sort of thing. I am sure that nobody ever bears witness, and it really doesn't matter. In essence, I have ended the season on my own terms."

Frank was also an optimist. "So far as this great bird is concerned," he wrote, "the elements are seldom hostile. Ruffed grouse conquered their environment centuries before any white man appeared on these shores. They are profligate enough to survive the attentions of wild predator and man. They retreat before the artificial lava flow of steel and cement, but they never concede victory while any fringe of woodland remains. If in the end of it, any game bird graces our wild lands, it will be the cocky, self-assured, and completely independent partridge of the north."

Developments in the thirty years since this book was published might have tempered Frank's optimism. Those who study grouse agree that their numbers are declining. Now the peaks in the well-certified population cycles of ruffed grouse barely reach what were, in Frank Woolner's best days afield, the valleys.

Certainly highways and housing developments have stolen habitat from the ruffed grouse. But biologists tell us that the greatest threat to healthy grouse populations is not the bulldozer or the chainsaw, and certainly not the man with a shotgun.

Grouse thrive in the tangly edges where woods meet fields. There they find shelter from their enemies as well as the grasses and grains and leaves and berries that make up their varied diet. The nineteenth-century New England farmers cleared the land, and when Frank began hunting grouse, he found the abandoned orchards and grapevine tangles, the old pastures grown to clumps of juniper and thornapple and edged with briar and brush, the cellarholes, graveyards, and stone walls, and the second-growth birch and poplar hillsides that the pioneers left behind. It all made ideal grouse cover.

Today, in spite of the encroachments of civilization, Frank Woolner's New England actually boasts more woodland than it did a century ago. But it's rapidly reverting to mature forest. Tall trees and a bare woodland floor make for poor grouse habitat.

If he would shoot predators to save grouse, Woolner surely would have approved of the pro-active approach of the Ruffed Grouse Society, which promotes selective clear-cutting to let the sunshine into the forest and create the openings and thick edges that attract grouse, thus intentionally mimicking what the settlers created inadvertently a century ago. "To be entirely effective in this highly technical age," he wrote presciently, "successful grouse management may have to be a massive undertaking—and an expensive one. Perhaps a development of forestry practices that will benefit timbermen and hunters alike is one possibility. This is no dream, and it may be realized in the foreseeable future. The knowledge acquired by game biologists in their trysts with failure will be put to good use as natural resources practices mesh for the common good of mankind."

Frank Woolner's life overlapped those of Burton L. Spiller, William Harnden Foster, and John Alden Knight, each of whom wrote timeless elegies to the ruffed grouse. Anybody who has read Spiller's *Grouse Feathers* and *More Grouse Feathers*, Foster's *New England Grouse Shooting*, or Knight's *The Ruffed Grouse* will agree that *Grouse Hunting Strategies* deserves an honored place on the bird-hunter's shelf alongside those classics. And those of us who savor his words and relish the autumn woodlands and thrill to the roar of the sudden flush can only hope that Woolner's plea for intelligent management of ruffed grouse habitat will be heeded.

"There is time" he wrote in 1970.

We fervently hope he was right.

—William G. Tapply
Pepperell, Massachusetts
December 1999

INTRODUCTION

*A*s this is written, early November has thinned our northern woodlands and it is quite possible to see a ruffed grouse for two or three fleeting seconds after the flush. I have a bird beside me, one of two raised this morning. He made the mistake of towering in white birches, and so he is mine—together with an immaculate memory.

Forewords, in spite of the connotation, usually are written after a book has been completed: they tie up loose ends and thank those whose brains the author has picked. Since I have read much that has been written about grouse, and since I have been blessed with good comrades in the field, I choose to begin at the beginning. Ergo, we are engaged with *Bonasa umbellus*.

In bookman's Latin, *Bonasa* likens the drumming of grouse to the bellowing of bison, and *umbellus* refers to that magnificent umbrella-like ruff that gives the bird part of its common name. There are vague subspecies of the clan, identified by nit-pickers through subtle color variations and tail-end-charlie Latin.

Personally, I develop no fever about subspecies. It is sufficient to know that ruffed grouse have been residents of this New World for more than 25,000 years: their bones are found in the middens of ancient man. They were a renewable resource and a delicacy before any European arrived on this continent.

Moreover, the grouse is highly adaptable. His range includes much of the north-central section of the United States–Canadian landmass, approximately thirty-four degrees of latitude from the Atlantic to the Pacific, or roughly half a continent. He is, and always has been, wild and self-sufficient. Only clean farming and the cement abortions of civilization drive him back, and he fights for every foot of terrain.

Let the fringe woodland return to any acre of viable land, and the partridge will also return.

In the beginning of American history our pioneers extolled the bird as both abundant and delicious. Because these Englishmen and *coureurs de bois* were far from home, they likened the species to the grouse, or *griais*, of their native lands, and so, of course, they called them "grouse."

But not for long. As early as 1630 the Puritans of the Massachusetts Bay Colony were speaking about partridges, again confusing them with an Old World species. To this day a New Englander refers to "pa'tridges" or pats, while gentlemen of our Mason-Dixon South yarn about pheasants, mountain pheasants, or mountain cocks.

Northward, away up in the border woodlands of Maine and in the Maritimes, residents prefer birch partridge, perhaps to differentiate between the fool hen or spruce grouse, a related species that never seems to learn that man is an enemy.

Across today's America, ruffed grouse, grouse, partridge—or simply pat—are equally popular as common names. Only the very ignorant refer to this wonderful bird as the *ruffled* grouse. True ruffled grouse are those I miss with a charge of chilled 8s, and I often think, in this case, that I am more ruffled than the bird.

It wasn't until 1750, long after pioneers had made the acquaintance of partridges, that bearded John Bartram essayed precise taxonomy. Bartram, that indefatigable naturalist, sent a specimen to England, together with much data concerning habits and habitat. Thereafter, savants agreed that the American bird was a unique new species.

Many men have written books about this ultimate creation. Indeed, throughout the history of upland gunning in America a surprising number of sportsmen have published personal paeans of praise, never intended for a mass market, but rather as expensive gifts for friends who had shared the delights of grouse hunting. Some of these works were remarkably well done, with passages equal to the best in upland literature. If they suffered any weakness it was a lack of basic information about the bird itself, quite understandable in view of the fact that each succeeding year finds more data available.

Hundreds of enthusiastic journalists have contributed to the sporting magazines, capsuling facts as they saw them during the wheeling years and, finally, a few skilled outdoor writers, people like Burton L. Spiller, William Harnden Foster, and John Alden Knight (the two latter deceased), produced important works. Their books are classics and I commend them to you.

Indeed, I am quite willing to crawl out upon a literary widow-maker to state that the cream of American grouse-hunting literature is represented by the works of Spiller, Foster, and Knight—in that order. The rest is a taster, with occasional magnificent short articles by such specialists as the late John C. Phillips. One wishes that Phillips had written more about partridges, for his knowledge of the bird was encyclopedic, and his writing style delightful.

Similarly, a recent Winchester-Western booklet called *Ruffed Grouse,* written by Winchester's very capable John Madson in 1969, is highly recommended. John is that rare bird, a first-rate game biologist, an enthusiastic upland hunter—and a gentleman who can hold his own in any company of writers.

In the field of life history, management, and propagation, towering over all, there is *The Ruffed Grouse,* a weighty and magnificent compendium of information authored by Gardiner Bump, Robert W. Darrow, Frank C. Edminster, and Walter F. Crissey. Those of us who delight in partridge hunting use this tremendous work as the final word in ecology, subject only to later research reported in the *Journal of Wildlife Management,* official publication of the Wildlife Society. ·

The Ruffed Grouse was published by the New York Conservation Department in 1947, but is now out of print. Originally priced at six dollars a copy, it was and is a most important work—worth considerably more if you are lucky enough to find one gathering dust in some metropolitan book shop.

Our premier grouse writers were, and those living are, zealots. They appear to have lived with and for this magnificent bird. Spiller's *Grouse Feathers* and *More Grouse Feathers* are sheer delight. William Harnden Foster's superlative *New England Grouse Shooting* was first published in 1942, yet his beliefs were pretty much those of today's bright young management technicians and hunters. So why another book on grouse?

For the first and most important reason on earth: mine is a love story, a sometimes personal treatise on the game bird that is more important to me than wild geese coursing an autumn sky, than black ducks cupping their wings and dropping into the blocks, than woodcock spiraling over the alders in the red hush of an October twilight.

And, finally, to bring this business up to date. There is nothing Gay

Burton L. Spiller and Tap Tapply converse at the edge of a grouse cover. Spiller has been called the "poet laureate of grouse hunting."

Ninetyish about the ruffed grouse. As a citizen, natural born, he progresses with the times and he scorns welfare. He is tough, cocky, adaptable, and fully prepared to get along without artificial propagation.

Nobody stocks grouse on a put-and-take basis. The bird competes with civilization, yet resists game-farm mass production. Modern aviculture has solved most of the problems concerned, yet partridges cannot be raised in sufficient numbers, at feasible costs, to justify massive release to the gun. Moreover, the artificially propagated bird seems to lose some of its inherent wildness. It is no wonder that few pats wear the subservient aluminum band that indicates game-farm origin.

I think it charitable to say that a man must walk as much as a mile for each grouse shot at. There are great years, of course, when birds are abundant and every laurel thicket or fox-grape tangle explodes as the brown bullets go drilling out. But there are doldrum periods as well, when pats are suffering one of their strange declines. Then woodlands seem barren and the miles march on without a flush.

Whatever the case, it is well to note that these are not level, unobstructed miles—they are country miles over rocky, overgrown, brierguarded side hills and ravines, through swamp edges where bogs are concealed by fallen leaves. You will hike the birch woods and struggle through junipers and bullbrier, breast laurel jungles and scrub oak thickets. You will pause to take a breather after steaming climbs to beech ridges and plateaus where mountain winds are keen in the pines and hemlocks. If you decide to hunt partridges, one thing is certain: you'll walk.

If this sounds like too much work, then I advise you to forget about pats and repair to the nearest public hunting ground where lesser birds are stocked in delightful little plots of barley and millet. There isn't as much challenge but, as in all things, a man must choose his particular level in sport.

The rewards of grouse hunting are enormous, and a heavy bag of game figures least of all. There is immense satisfaction in prospecting new covers and in further study of those that have become familiar over the years. One savors the wonderful musk of the wilderness, a blend of leaf mold and evergreen, juniper and the clean bite of spruce gum. In late November, after the leaves have fallen and the first ice crystals are stitching quiet pools, there is always a faint scent of skunk in the woodlands: I hold it pleasant.

Upland hunters absorb the wonders of nature and their dreams are full of hawks' cries and strange little gardens in the woods. Who else properly appreciates the velvet spikes of sumac glowing in the orange light of autumn? Who but a grouse hunter can really savor the lavender gold wash of color that tints a stand of hardwoods in the late afternoon of a November day?

If we pause to munch wintergreen berries, or tarry to examine a muskrat's lodge—built much too close to a swamp's edge and therefore subject to the immediate attention of trappers—we are not wasting time, but adding to a vast store of knowledge and delight. It is a good thing to get away from the great cities, to employ scent and sight and hearing, to somehow feel the presence of the aboriginal Indians and the pioneers long gone from this harried planet.

The partridge hunter is all-American, and he is a true perfectionist. He seeks a game bird that has been called the greatest—simply because it is completely wild and very difficult to kill with any degree of consistency. Grouse are far from exotic: they are plentiful enough to startle millions of farm boys, yet the bird has become a status trophy. Beginners are enthralled by this grandest of flying targets, yet a legion of middle-aged marksmen offer the supreme accolade: they mean grouse, and grouse only, when they speak of "birds."

Among this latter group are: Horace G. "Tap" Tapply, the well-known outdoor writer and editor; Hal Lyman, publisher of *Salt Water Sportsman* Magazine; Bill Pollack, chief game biologist of the Massachusetts Division of Fisheries and Game; and my brothers, Jack and Dick Woolner. All are grouse hunters, and that should be description enough.

Finally, and with tongue only partially in cheek, I must express thanks to the various divisions of fisheries and game for stocking multitudes of ring-necked pheasants. May they prosper, for they keep those ever-increasing legions of comfort-loving neo-outdoorsmen out of coverts frequented by true game birds.

I am all for the pheasant, a great gaudy gladiator that lumbers out of low brush like a helicopter with a broken rotor, and teaches a standard of gunnery far below that necessary to score consistently on the royalty of upland game.

*T*he ruffed grouse, grouse, partridge, or pat is a gallinaceous fowl of our New World. To a pedant it is: order *Gallinae;* suborder *Phasiani;* family *Tetraonidae;* species *Bonasa umbellus.*

Precise taxonomists recognize at least eleven different subspecies of grouse, distinguished by lighter or darker plumage, with size and weight an additional factor. These slight variations are of little concern to the sportsman or casual student of natural history. All American ruffed grouse, to a layman's eye, are remarkably alike.

An adult is roughly eighteen inches in length, from dainty beak to square-tail tip, and weighs approximately one and one-half pounds. Occasional birds may push two pounds, although such portly individuals are rare. Males are heavier than females, but the difference is slight.

Both sexes display the ruff, which may be iridescent black or bronzed, depending on color phase. Both wear a topknot or crest upon their heads, and both display the characteristic fantail—usually eighteen to twenty square-tipped feathers. (If it matters, an average grouse wears an overall total of 4,300 to 4,500 feathers, not including down.)

Sexing is tricky, for there are no easily determined exterior markers. If there is any rule of thumb, apply the generally accepted male-female standards of masculinity and femininity. Hen grouse are lighter in weight, more delicately fashioned, and more subtly marked. Cocks are bigger, brasher, and brighter colored; their tail feathers are longer and their ruffs more prominent.

Length of tail feathers is a good indication of sex. Usually, but not always, the bird that boasts tail feathers of 5⅞ inches or longer is a male. Usually, and again not always, the dark terminal band on the

Grouse in display attitude. PHOTO BY SCOTT–SWEDBERG

Tap Tapply displays cock and hen grouse, left and right. Longer tail and unbroken black band distinguishes cock. Tail of hen is much shorter, and terminal band usually is broken.

tail feathers of a male will be almost continuous, unbroken by the two central shafts that, in the hen, often lack this distinctive band.

Immature birds naturally present greater obstacles to instant sexing, but examination of wing tips should distinguish the young from the adult. In a bird of the year, ninth and tenth primaries (outermost flight feathers) will be sharply pointed, while those of the old bird— second year and thereafter—will be rounded. As a further check, juveniles display sheath remnants at the bases of their seventh and eighth primaries, but not their ninth and tenth. Adults, contrarily, show sheath remnants on ninth and tenth primaries.

Every grouse fancier is impressed by the subtle beauty of a partridge. From gently barred brown-and-white breast to regal fantail, this is a superb creation. The spear-patterned feathers of back and rump, although tinted warm brown, cream, and fawn, always remind me of royal ermine. Generations of upland gunners have elevated their souls simply by admiring the rich, conservative plumage of freshly acquired grouse. How often have we all paused to stroke those soft feathers, to spread the impossible fantail to its uttermost limits, and to marvel at perfection in camouflage coupled with functional beauty.

The dominant color of an adult grouse is gray or gray brown to almost brick red, with subtle color gradients between the three. Natural selection has given the bird of the far north more gray than red, for this flyer lives much of its life in an environmental pattern of dark shadows. Red phases become more pronounced in central and southern ranges, hence the so-called red ruff is more likely to be seen in southern New England, Pennsylvania, and Virginia than in Canada. Color varies between red and gray in central New England, while northern birds—from the Atlantic Maritimes to Michigan's Upper Peninsula and across the breadth of the cold lands to Alaska's Yukon Valley—generally are clothed in gray.

Trout fishing and grouse hunting, although diametrically opposed, are kindred arts—perhaps because trout and grouse have become symbolic as the most sporting representatives of American angling and gunning. The soft, subtly marked hackle of a partridge lends itself to the creation of such traditional trout flies as the March Brown. Romance spices life when a man ties his own flies with the feathers of a magnificent bird honorably taken, and then proceeds to tempt a coveted game fish with the resultant artificial.

Partridges are feathered to a point just above the foot, and the foot is wonderfully adapted to provide support at all seasons. In late summer and early fall each toe sprouts fringes of tiny, chitinous rods that are so small as to be hardly discernible. As cold weather descends upon northern woodlands these fringes grow rapidly and provide the bird with greater bearing surface. Thus the grouse wears snowshoes when these are necessary for survival, and sheds its webs in the spring.

American Indians once forecast the severity of a coming winter by noting the autumnal development of snowshoes on the feet of grouse. I am not going to embrace medicine-man biology, but it is true that the growth rate of these appendages varies considerably from year to year. It would be pleasant to believe that partridges can predict a winter's snowfall, yet we know only that some marvelous internal chemistry triggers a growth function where it is needed. One day some bright research technician will discover how it is done—and another lovely little legend will fall before the guns of hard science.

Our grouse, on its home ground, is rarely the fan-tailed, spectacularly ruffed, and bulky creation of sporting magazines and identification manuals. With the exception of those periods when a male is strutting to impress a female or to intimidate another male, the pat is sleek and functional. Both sexes are slim, taut, proud in carriage, with feathers slicked down as though varnished. Only in cold weather,

Snowshoe fringes on a grouse's foot are already beginning to be shed by this Massachusetts bird, killed by a motorcar in March.

when there is a need for insulation, will the grouse fluff up and appear twice its natural size.

The dyspeptic motorcycle beat of spring drumming is a familiar sound in partridge coverts, yet few know that our pat employs a considerable vocabulary. Birds communicate in all seasons, using a few basic sounds that are varied by inflection. Perhaps most familiar is the rapid "peep-peep-peep" of a grouse surprised by dog or man, usually uttered as the bird prepares to flush.

There are inquiry, distress, and warning notes. Often a female with chicks will squeal, and both sexes are given to occasional hissing. Hens scold their youngsters with curt clucks and reassure them with a soft, cooing sound. Adults, male and female, often indulge in a questioning note, a sort of "crr-eck," with accent on the second syllable.

While male birds may drum during any month of the year, the act is a sexual manifestation and therefore most often undertaken during the vernal equinox. Trout fishermen, for years beyond recollection, have paused in the bright mornings and tawny afternoons to admire these bongo drums of springtime.

A drumming "log" may be anything from an actual log to a stump, a hummock, or a boulder. However, where true logs are reasonably abundant they are preferred—and the same log will be used year after year. Since grouse are remarkably short-lived, successive cocks must instinctively recognize an ideal location for drum talk. The curiously ventriloquistic sound is produced by beating the wings against the air, much as a human being claps hands. Slow-motion

Cock grouse strutting on drumming log. PHOTO BY SCOTT–SWEDBERG

photography proves, however, that wing tips are not brought together.

Not only are specific logs chosen by successive generations of birds, but each drummer seems to pick the same spot to begin his performance. Wings akimbo, tail spread, and ruff prominent, he struts back and forth, pauses, carefully assures his footing, and then stands erect like a pouter pigeon, his half-spread tail providing a measure of balance.

Then, quickly, those powerful wings sweep forward and up to produce the first echoing thump. Another thump—and then a rapid acceleration until individual wingbeats merge into a strange blur of thunder. In this manner a cock grouse proclaims sovereignty over a territory he has claimed, warns all other males to keep their distance, and invites hens to admire a champion.

Unfortunately the sound stimulates foes as well as potential mates. Foxes, goshawks, and other predators take birds while they are ad-

Cock grouse on a drumming log. PHOTO BY SCOTT–SWEDBERG

vertising their virility. Evidently the partridge is aware of this danger, for a grouse on a drumming log is highly alert and more than usually spooky. It requires superior skill in stalking to approach and observe a performer: those who have photographed the act deserve highest commendation.

Jack Swedberg and Carl Scott of Millbury, Massachusetts, two capable outdoor motion-picture producers, have observed and photographed drumming grouse on many occasions. They have discovered that a bird may approach a drumming log as early as 3:00 A.M. and occasionally takes station at midnight.

Swedberg and Scott have also noted that drumming requires practice. Birds of the year try to produce the thunderous challenge, but often fail. They assume the proper stance, clap their wings mightily— and produce no sound! This, for a proud bird, must be humiliating.

Some cocks drum throughout the year and any performance in the fall may lead a gunner to good sport. If a challenger sends his roll of thunder through the autumn woodlands, he is more likely to attract combative males than eager females. Thus a strutting, musically inclined grouse usually means others of his kind in the immediate vicinity.

Some grouse cannot resist investigating any noise remotely similar to the drums of spring. Hens and cocks have been known to patter alongside a slowly moving truck, cocking their heads to listen to the sound of an internal combustion engine. Audubon wrote of tolling in pats by beating upon an inflated pig's bladder. Anyone for a patent grouse call?

Our great game bird is fiercely combative. Cocks invariably challenge their own sex and often intimidate females. A few wags, tongue in cheek, have suggested that these birds can't tell the difference between sexes. I am *not* going to suggest that this may be a reason for periods of scarcity!

There is a definite pecking order in grouse coverts, with intimidation or actual combat deciding superiority. The former consists of strutting with tail spread wide, ruff flared, and wings drooping. There is a great deal of headshaking and hissing, guttural warning clucks, and jerky movement.

Actual belligerents assume an entirely different pose. The fighting stance is almost reptilian. Birds lower their heads, extend their necks, tighten feathers close to their bodies, and circle warily. Then they close with a feathery rush, pecking, scratching, and buffeting with their wings. In game-farm pens, unless quickly separated, the weaker is almost sure to be scalped. However, it is rather unlikely that wild grouse kill one another, because a vanquished or intimidated bird will retreat before it is seriously injured.

In the spring a grouse's fancy, as in a majority of living things, turns to the miracle of reproduction. Yet strangely, as though this fiercely stimulated bird were completely baffled by the ecstasy that generates display and drumming, the male may take no immediate interest when a brown biddy (statistically almost always a virgin) appears. In turn, she seems drawn by invisible and incomprehensible wires to this strutting, thundering colossus, but dodges any advance.

For a time, aside from strutting, hissing, and headshaking, he ignores her. Then, as the mating urge pounds in his blood, the cock grouse begins to follow his chosen mate. Coyly, she evades him, even fluttering into the treetops to keep her lover at a proper distance. Furious, he drums with renewed vigor, struts, and hisses venomously. She preens her feathers, adroitly steps aside and, like any coquette, tempts him.

Finally, as the warmth of springtime increases, there is a day when the male sheds his belligerence and becomes curiously gentle. Now he is a mooning, silent romantic, a prisoner of love. The hen ignores him and he follows her silently, slowly, the very epitome of unrequited passion. Indeed, he sings to her, a soft, cooing note. Spring sunshine filters through suddenly green leaves. The earth sends up its heady perfume, and eventually she responds, squatting, assuming the mating position. He places an immaculate foot on her outstretched tail.

Perhaps, on this first gentle contact, the hen will struggle free and proceed to tease her frustrated Lothario. He follows passively, utterly bewitched until that climactic moment when his mate responds and the two are joined.

Having mated, the cock grouse takes no further interest in either the hen or her progeny. He does not aid in the incubation of eggs or in the rearing of a brood. Instead, he reverts to strutting and fighting, maintaining his position in the pecking order of grousedom. Normally polygamous, a male may woo several hens, but he is most discerning. Hybridization is rare.

The female grouse lays an average clutch of ten to twelve eggs (although as many as nineteen have been found) in a primitive depression scratched out at the base of a stump, a tree trunk, or in the edge of a brush pile. Observers have reported clutches in such exotic

Grouse nest and eggs at the edge of a brushpile.

locations as old crows' nests and the interior of hollow stumps. Almost always the nest will be in or adjacent to a brushy clearing. The buff-color eggs, somewhat smaller than a golf ball and spotted with olive drab to reddish flecks, normally hatch in twenty-three and a half days.

In some cases a hen partridge seems instinctively to know when an egg is infertile, and she will discard that one by kicking it out of the nest. Again, there are occasions when she will brood for the entire period, and then leave a hopeless clutch. Several years ago I watched and photographed a hen that brooded for twenty-two days, during which time six of the original ten eggs disappeared. The remaining four were deserted at the end of it, and examination proved that they were infertile. Such a bird may mate again and produce a late brood. These are the underprivileged half-grown pullets sometimes harvested by gunners in the autumn.

Almost immediately upon chipping the shell, grouse chicks are mobile. They are yellow-brown atoms of vibrant life, fully prepared to scamper through the understory and feed themselves. From the very beginning they recognize the hen's warning notes and will freeze at a signal, or emerge to feast and frolic.

Folklore insists that partridge chicks always hide under a leaf, but I think this romantic nonsense. Occasionally one may freeze in a position where a leaf covers its tiny body, but the hen's warning usually triggers one single response: the chick becomes completely immobile, flattened against the earth, trusting its natural camouflage. The result is astonishing: these fluffy gnomes melt into a patchwork of growing plants, leaf mold, and shadow. One moment you see a scurrying flock of little ones, and then—nothing. It is wise to step carefully, for it is too easy to tramp upon a motionless chick.

Surprised at the nest, a female ruffed grouse usually will flush and disappear into surrounding woodlands, to return when she feels that the interloper has departed. At this time a broody bird is unlikely to work the broken-wing trick. Startle her when fluffy immatures are combing the ground for food, and you'll see a real production. The hen may emit an initial squeal, together with a few warning clucks— intended to send her children into hiding. Thereafter she will act out the part of a disabled bird, fluttering along the ground and appearing to be easy prey for dog or human. Her object, of course, is to decoy predators away from her flock.

Occasionally a hen grouse will attack an encroacher. Biddies have been known to fly at the head of a man, a dog, or a skulking red fox. This is unusual, but far from rare. Such birds, together with those feigning incapacitation, are often captured by swift foxes, dogs, and cats. Wild predators snap up a fair share of playacting or combative pats, after which they retrace their steps to devour the chicks. For all of that, the sudden battering attack and the broken-wing capers are good tricks, and they probably save many broods.

For their part, the tiny grouse remain frozen for so long as movement, sound, or shadow threatens danger. When woodlands are quiet they soon become restive and begin to peep—a thin, reedy little sound, usually three notes in descending order. They come scurrying as the hen returns and calls them back to her side.

Partridge chicks must have relatively open coverts during their first weeks of life. Low brush is their domain, even though canopied woodlands will prove more attractive in later months. Now they need the huckleberry edges and the wild clearings that have begun to sprout new growth. They must have insects and fleshy fruits, tender grasses and other vegetation. Sunlight and warmth and dust baths are imperative. For a couple of weeks, at night and in inclement weather, they'll be hovered by the biddy.

Curiously, in view of the adult's predominantly vegetarian diet, grouse chicks consume many insects during the first ten days of their life. Ants are taken with great relish and a whole host of invertebrates become fair game. The insects provide fats and proteins that are essential to growth. Evidently dewdrops and succulent vegetation provide enough moisture. Indeed, except in game-farm pens, few have witnessed grouse in the act of drinking. Possibly ground water is utilized, and it may be that fruits and buds provide sufficient moisture.

Our partridge matures rapidly. The chick of early May will flutter to a perch on a low branch at one week of age, and he'll buzz over the huckleberries at three weeks. This is a precarious flight, far from the hipper-dipper aerobatics of November, but this fledgling of the woodlot is already testing its wings. By late summer all the birds are close to maturity, although juveniles are still small and lack the cunning of their elders. Time now becomes an implacable enemy, for the grouse will be lucky indeed to observe a first birthday. A great majority will be gone within a year, and practically all after two seasons.

Wild partridges are hardly blessed by longevity. While there is record of a penned bird that survived to the extreme old age of seven-

A ten-week-old ruffed grouse forages in early-summer ground cover. PHOTO
BY SANFORD W. SCHEMNITZ

teen, in the wilderness a pat is an old-timer at two, and a three- or
four-year-old is ancient. Unless your thinking is relative, "Old Ruff"
is a figment of imagination, and the sportsman who yarns about a specific bird that has been eluding him for ten years is a mite confused.

Mortality in the wild is formidable, without gunning. During the
course of a single year it is estimated that half the birds accumulated
by a successful nesting season will disappear. Michigan's biologists
have placed over-winter mortality at "a normal" 70 percent of available
stock.

Mid-September through early October is the time of fall shuffle or
crazy flight. Then broods of the year break up, with individuals seeking new coverts. Grouse, at this time, fly through plate-glass windows,
dash themselves to death against various immovable objects, and generally behave as though courting suicide.

Many theories have been advanced to explain this phenomenon.
The Indians of aboriginal America assumed that all partridges go crazy
in the fall—hence "crazy flight" is a time-honored phrase. This is a
colorful deduction, but it has proved erroneous. Modern game biologists have found that practically all birds killed in the early-fall shuffle
are immatures.

Imaginative outdoorsmen have wondered whether the brilliant colors of fall foliage might frighten birds. Falling leaves, they reason, might well perplex the young of the year and trigger those seemingly frantic flights that too often end in disaster.

For the crazy-flight pat that acts like a drunkard on a spree, there is the perennial explanation: fermented fruits. If a milch cow can become a sot on cider apples, why is it not entirely reasonable to assume that a bird may go on a similar bender?

For many years I toyed with the idea that fall shuffle might be the result of dining on hallucinatory fungi. We know that grouse eat mushrooms and that they can tolerate foods that would prove fatal if consumed by a human being. No research findings are available, but most of the facts appear to deny my pet theory.

Crazy flight, it seems to me, is nature's way of dispersing broods and introducing new blood into suitable covers anywhere from a mile to more than five miles from point of origin. There is a spring shuffle, too, but this is never so hectic a scattering as the autumn phenomenon and it is accomplished with far fewer losses.

Still, inquisitive sportsmen would like to know whether crazy flight

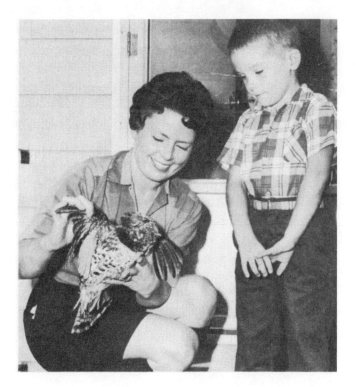

A crazy-flight grouse, killed by smashing through a window.

is initiated only when covers are overcrowded, and whether the young of the year are actually hastened on their way by adults. Again, the evidence would seem to dispute this hypothesis. Game biologists have noted that, even in pens, young birds become increasingly nervous as autumn approaches. Something in their nature senses a change, a need to break away from natal coverts and to establish new hierarchies of grousedom. Crazy flight is a transitional madness, the natural rebellion of the young that courts disaster as it bridges the dangerous gap between youth and adulthood. We have, as human beings, experienced our own periods of crazy flight.

Periodically, outdoor writers produce articles that guarantee a hunter's success if he will only study the foods that grouse eat, and then hie himself to the nearest banquet table. One must always, according to these advisers, slit the crop of a freshly downed bird in order to determine its tastes. If there is logic in the approach, it escapes me. Granting that the ruffed grouse can be selective, one must also admit that its taste is catholic. A partridge eats almost any vegetable matter that is remotely edible, plus some forage that we humans view with logical alarm.

It would be futile, or at least encyclopedic, to list the many delicacies consumed by this bird: they include a multitude of buds, berries, fruits, seeds, mast, leaves, grasses, and tender shoots. Insects, although an infinitesimal percentage of adult grouse diet, are consumed, and mushrooms may serve as dessert. Some of the fungi ingested by our royal game bird would propel a human being into a hospital bed, and possibly into a plot of ground where perpetual care is promised by survivors.

To confound those who suggest the selective feeding approach— and to further confound myself—I have bagged successive birds that seemed to have enjoyed a smorgasbord. Example: In a bag of three collected in a single covert during one sunny afternoon, Grouse 1 had a crop full of acorns, together with traces of mushrooms; Grouse 2 had been quenching its hunger and thirst with pigeon grapes; Grouse 3 (and mind you all these birds were shot in the same area) was practically bursting with wintergreen, acorns, aspen buds, bits of apple leaves, and the berries of poison ivy.

Fortunately, poison ivy has never bothered me. As an insufferable youth I even chewed the shiny green leaves to impress contemporaries, and I escaped punishment. However, there are documented cases of sportsmen contracting the infernal itch after dressing birds and coming into contact with poison ivy berries in crops or gizzards.

Ingestion of such toxic substances—including mountain laurel, poison sumac, and bittersweet—has been said to affect the flesh of the bird. Although folklore holds that a laurel-eating pat may sicken a human being, no modern research has proved it so.

I think the ruffed grouse is far less selective than many of us would like to believe. He feeds on the available, and the available is legion. Partridges have prospered for so long in our sometimes inhospitable north-central climes that they can consume and digest almost any vegetable matter. There is reason to believe that grouse never go hungry.

Obviously, with a bow to those who place their trust in selective feeding, the cornucopia of goodies depends on region and season. Birds of the Great Smokies find a different array of vegetation from those of Canada's Maritime Provinces and Michigan's Upper Peninsula. Moreover, all grouse are forced to switch from succulent ground-bearing fruits, such as strawberries and blackberries, to summer fruits and seeds and buds as the inexorable seasons roll. A great variety of leaves and tender shoots are consumed. Aspen is a more or less universal food, often present in areas where pats are abundant.

Game biologists are now convinced that the adult bird is selective to an extreme where aspen is concerned. Recently Dr. Sanford D. Schemnitz, professor of wildlife resources at the University of Maine, writing about winter feeding, declared that grouse observed during a Down East winter research project "fed totally on male aspen trees with their large clustered buds and avoided female aspen trees with their small scattered buds." Other game biologists concur with Dr. Schemnitz.

The fact that this great bird is a budder has generated much controversy. Several of the New England states have experimented with bounties on grouse because these birds insist upon raiding apple orchards. Various Eastern states have paid orchardists for real or imagined damage. Ripe fruits are readily taken, but this presents no burning problem, for late summer and fall fodder consists mainly of windfalls.

In many eastern regions, shooters are convinced that good sport depends upon a bumper crop of apples. Therefore, in late years, there has been some grumbling about clean orchard practices that leave no

Grouse budding white birch at West Old Town, Maine. PHOTO BY HOWARD PARKER

understory to protect the birds, and much vitriolic comment on the effects of insecticides. Laboratory analysis has turned up varying amounts of DDT in the bodies of grouse, yet no conclusions have been reached. After all, every living thing upon this earth now carries a residue of man-made poison.

Usually, apples that feed grouse are the fruits of stunted old trees away back in the puckerbrush. These are the descendants of pioneer orchards and they have never known a toxic spray. Their tart, worm-riddled fruit plummet to the ground with September's line storms and there, in the shadow and shine of protective cover, are sought by partridges. Curiously, particular trees—apparently identical to others in the immediate vicinity—are most attractive to grouse.

Tap Tapply is firmly convinced that pats prefer red apples to green or yellow ones, having observed the phenomenon throughout a life-time of shooting. I am not convinced, but this is something to think about. Perhaps color is important: Certainly some birds and some fishes are excited by brilliant hues. Since pats eat quantities of apple leaves, especially in the late fall—and prefer certain trees over others—the mystery is compounded.

Generally speaking, our royal game bird—after crazy flight and spring shuffle—seems to live its life out in a small territory, probably a mixture of cover not exceeding one hundred acres. Depending on seasons and weather conditions, particular sections of this range are most heavily utilized. In high summer, for example, birds often retire to thick swamp edges while they are in the process of moulting.

If one hundred acres of living room pleases the average partridge, it should be noted that in successive years, each terminated by crazy flight, much larger areas are populated. Michigan's game biologists have declared that birds will disperse over at least one hundred square miles during a four-year period, and it is common knowledge that good cover will draw grouse from considerable distances. All this indicates a rather plastic definition of range.

Ornithologists declare that the pat is nonmigratory, yet some great woodsmen disagree. There are recurring tales of huge flocks raised in hitherto poor to mediocre coverts. Invariably, according to these accounts, the birds move rapidly and seldom allow themselves to be approached by following shooters. I have never observed the phenomenon, yet I have discussed the matter with gunners not given to wild exaggerations and they say they have observed such mass flights.

So far as the record is concerned, there is no documented evidence of true migration and there seems adequate proof that sustained flight over land is impossible. For one thing, experiments appear to have proved that a partridge cannot remain airborne for so short a distance as one mile over water. It logically follows that sustained flight over land is a much shorter journey than our folklore would indicate.

Excited hunters and awe-inspired countrymen have always yarned about birds that flushed and flew right over the horizon. Actually, normal grouse flight is likely to encompass something between one hundred and two hundred yards—and the latter would be a long trip, possibly accomplished in slanting down the face of a hill. Much longer flights, some of which may actually exceed that minus-one-mile limit, are perhaps feasible when a bird flushes in a gale and is thereby enabled to ride a near-surface jet stream.

On Scottish moors, gamekeepers live in constant fear that a howling wind may push red grouse right out of the country. Similarly, there is a possibility that an American partridge may find itself buoyed up by a wind under its tail and may thereby scale for an astonishing distance. All of us who hunt grouse have seen occasional cases wherein a bird will continue to fan its wings on a long, high, and apparently level course. In this case thermals and high winds undoubtedly aid the flyer. Perhaps the bird is a victim of air currents, destined to alight in a foreign covert.

It is now believed that a grouse attains forty to fifty miles an hour in level flight and that this velocity may be attained right from blast-off. "Level flight" is not a good phrase to use, but I think "blast-off," to describe the flush, is surprisingly apt. Like one of our ballistic missiles, much of this bird's spectacular energy is expended in an initial burst of turbulence as it leaves the ground and accelerates up over the rising curve of a parabolic trajectory. Like the rocket, it creates a great deal of fuss during one split second of lift-off, accelerates rapidly, and attains maximum flying speed just as it reaches the top of that heroic arc. Thereupon, a grouse usually becomes more missile than flying machine: it trims down to an aerodynamically perfect silhouette, neck extended, plumage flattened, wings cupped and swept back. Speed remains constant, or may even increase as the partridge slants down in a shallow dive.

Those who are fortunate enough to see a bird midway in its precipitous passage through heavy cover will marvel at the split-second timing that avoids collision with tree trunks or heavy branches. Near at hand you will hear the hiss of air through primaries and tail feathers as course changes are executed. Twigs may be clipped by this living projectile, but disaster is rare. The grouse is a master of aerial slalom.

Occasionally, though, a partridge will spear itself on a treacherous stub. Birds have been discovered with shafts of hardwood imbedded in their breasts and nicely healed over. Whether these were driven home during the reckless crazy flight of early fall or were the result of adult pilot error is unknown.

At flush, evasive tactics may be more important than speed. An adult instinctively seems to place the nearest bush, tree, or terrain feature between its line of flight and the observer. If brush is low-growing, a pat usually flies just over root level. In evergreens, he dodges behind the first screening conifer and departs triumphantly. In woodland cover there is a tendency for males to tower in a swift, climbing turn, while biddies are more likely to execute a shallow, rising trajectory.

Some pats, cock or hen, are given to flushing and flying for no more than a few yards. Some flit off silently, close to the ground. A few— and probably more than we suspect—never flush at all: they run ahead of an approaching gunner or dog and, unless the terrain makes flight necessary, never take to the air.

In any event, the whir of a partridge's flush has unstrung generations of would-be killers. This thunderous getaway is ideally suited to jangle the nerves of any anxious predator, man or beast. With forty years of shooting behind me, I still get flustered by the upsetting clamor of a pat's departure. Lord, let that emotion remain!

Camouflage is another of our great bird's defensive weapons. In thickets, where grouse search for low-lying food, movement or sound betrays them, but rarely form or color. Often I have had pats approach me while I was posting for deer or a red fox running ahead of hounds. First the noise of the bird, scratching and questing like the chicken of the woods that it is; then movement; and, finally, the slim, taut form stepping proudly. A grouse is a part of the woodlands, a sprite of the American wilderness.

Roosting in a stunted wild apple or pine tree, the partridge seems to blend into trunk and branch structure. It can be startling when a simulated stub suddenly roars off and goes slanting down in a tumultuous dive.

Cocky, combative, and beautifully adapted to life in the boreal and transitional forests of North America, the ruffed grouse remains a delicate, high-strung bird, heir to difficulties both known and unknown. Of these limiting factors, the so-called cycle is most familiar. Supposedly, pats build to a population peak in nine years (or seven, or twelve, depending on local conviction), after which there is a corresponding decline for the same period.

Unfortunately for those with tidy mathematical minds, our birds seldom cooperate. Certainly there are fluctuations in population, with up or down trends spread over a number of years. However, there is no sharply etched periodicity, and to be truly cyclic, this would have to be established. Moreover, the cycle is far from constant. Birds may diminish in one area, and increase in another. The theory remains an escape for those who still labor in the labyrinths of ecology and it is questioned by erudite biologists.

Grouse in deep winter, during an ice storm.

Since it has been demonstrated that an extremely cold, wet nesting and brooding season can thin the grouse population of any given area, one or a series of poor brood years may well be responsible for a sudden decline. Given ideal conditions, it would then take approximately four breeding seasons to produce a new peak. This logic is inescapable if you accept the fact that normal mortality, from one year to the next *under good conditions,* is as high as 70 percent.

Disease may be a factor in any decline, and predation subtracts a reasonably well-documented percentage. Automobiles kill grouse, particularly when birds are crossing country roads from cover to cover. You will find that generation after generation of pats will use the same crossing spots until such time as topographical change roadblocks a traditional run.

Pats reared by game biologists have proved highly susceptible to various poultry diseases. Parasitism is common, with worms and ticks preying on apparently healthy birds. Sportsmen often discover wiry, intestinal roundworms while dressing their quarry, and there are others that a hunter rarely sees, because they are small and well hidden. Tough-bodied, lethargic winged grouse ticks often appear in the plumage of recently downed game.

Worth noting is the fact that no biologist has yet uncovered evidence that disease or excessive parasitism is a major factor in the fluctuation of grouse populations. Nonetheless, scientists continue to

Fluffed up against the cold, grouse forages when buds are covered with ice.

explore the problem, and there is a possibility that they will come up with new findings and solutions.

The challenge is tremendous, if only because grouse are subject to population explosions and equally precipitous declines. Any living creature capable of multiplying itself at a prodigious rate is subject to corresponding massive mortality. Given ideal conditions a brace of grouse could theoretically produce 33,000 descendants in the short period of four years. These are the boom and bust children of nature.

Michigan's game biologists have found that subnormal temperatures in springtime may exact an inordinate toll of hens, as well as chicks. Aside from this, there is little evidence that adults are unduly dismayed by heat, cold, flood, or snowstorm—excepting as these extremes favor predation. A silver thaw that covers every twig with a glass-hard coating may annoy them for several days, but starvation is unlikely for a species that thrives on so great a variety of buds, berries, seeds, and wild fruits.

I am convinced that a partridge senses changes in barometric pressures that presage a storm. On several perfectly lovely midwinter mornings, when there was no wind of consequence and the temperature was well above freezing, I have noted the complete absence of fresh grouse tracks, but have flushed birds out of ground roosting forms. Although much field study would be necessary to confirm the opinion, it is logical to suspect that birds may postpone foraging to

Winter is no great terror for grouse, because the species feeds on a great variety of buds. PHOTO BY LEONARD LEE RUE III

prepare for approaching bad weather. In each case of those I mention, a heavy snowstorm actually began within five hours.

Grouse often roost in thick conifers during a snowfall, but many prefer to remain on the ground. These earth-loving birds allow themselves to be buried when temperatures are low enough to ensure a dry, powdery coating. They use snow as insulation and may remain entombed for hours.

Partridges are known to fly straight into snowbanks or, if they happen to be walking, to burrow under the surface, usually to a depth just sufficient to afford cover and warmth. Surprised by man, or by any four-footed predator, they burst straight up through the snow, apparently in full flight from the moment of lift-off.

Legend holds that grouse may truly be entombed by crust, so that they die of starvation under the hard covering. Modern biologists never deny that this may occur, but there is no documented account of a bird found so imprisoned. If it indeed happens, this must be a rare occurrence.

So far as this great bird is concerned, the elements are seldom hostile. Ruffed grouse conquered their environment centuries before any white man appeared on these shores. They are profligate enough to survive the attentions of wild predator and man. They retreat before the artificial lava flow of steel and cement, but they never concede victory while any fringe woodland remains. If in the end of it, any game bird graces our wild lands, it will be the cocky, self-assured, and completely independent partridge of the north.

TWO • TOOTH, CLAW, AND HOOF

*I*t is characteristic of well-meaning yet ill-informed nature lovers to insist that all predators are beneficial because they exist on a steady diet of rats, mice, insects, or whatever is currently deemed an enemy of mankind. This product of wishful thinking contains just enough truth to make it dangerous.

On the other side of the cover, extremists who rant that every flesh-eating bird or mammal should be shot on sight betray an abject ignorance of wildlife dynamics. Predation is a necessary fact of life: it is a natural means by which surpluses are removed so that any given species can exist in a habitat niche. Normal removal culls out aged or diseased individuals. Logically, the survivors are sturdy and healthy, the elite brood stock on which the future well-being of a species depends.

There is no doubt that most of the tooth and claw tribes capture more mice than songbirds and ruffed grouse, but this preponderance of rodents in predator diet is based on the abundance of small buffer species rather than on selectivity. No fox, great horned owl, or goshawk ever declined a dinner of fresh partridges.

These three, together with the common house cat and weasel, are major killers: they are aided and abetted by a host of lesser marauders; yet it is worth noting that no rapacious bird or mammal specializes in the slaughter of grouse. All take birds and eggs as targets of opportunity; therefore rigid control becomes necessary only when nature's balance is upset and predators become abnormally abundant.

Foxes are highly intelligent marauders of our woodlands. Some think them an ultimate threat to grouse, but I hold this emotional generalization. No study has ever indicated wholesale murder of pats by foxes, though they do kill birds.

Often in midwinter, when there is tracking snow, I like to trudge over hills and ridges, through swamp edges and conifers. Sometimes I carry a target pistol in a shoulder holster—why I cannot tell you, unless it is to feel armed in the wilderness. Of course this is ridiculous where the "wilderness" consists of abandoned farmlands and hardwood ridges within sight and sound of suburbia.

Invariably the gun remains in its holster and I spend a wonderful afternoon reading thrillers in the snow. One story is forever repeated and, depending upon one's point of view, tells of tragedy or triumph.

There are the fox tracks—neat, straightforward, quartering cover professionally. I always nod with approval when I find that point where the red wraith had halted, pounced sidewise and pinned a mouse in a tuft of dead grass. There are the tracks of the fox, and those of the mouse—proceeding so far, no farther. A few drops of crimson and a minuscule fluff of gray-brown fur tell the tale.

Later, the snow offers another script as those fastidious fox prints overlap the fussy, little-old-lady track of a grouse. The plot thickens and I find myself reconstructing this drama. Apparently a partridge, tucked into a conifer during yesterday's storm, had plunged down at twilight to forage through this thicket. Finally, as skies cleared and sunset faded, the bird had burrowed into a drift, hollowed out a chamber, and prepared to roost.

The fox tracks became stealthy. There was a point at which he had crouched, almost at full length, savoring the fine aroma of grouse sifting out of a miniature air hole. Anyone with a smattering of imagination might see the rest of it in that padded depression that still contained a few feathers and a dye of crimson, but not one atom of flesh or bone. A fox had stalked, leaped, and secured his victim in a bomb burst of flying snow and thrashing wings.

And so, one less partridge. But I have also noticed that foxes often miss the birds they have so carefully hunted. One finds the same careful approach, culminating in a heroic leap—beyond which the lift-off pattern of wings is evident. I wonder whether an unsuccessful fox is chagrined, angry at himself? More likely he watches the departing bird, curls his tongue out in a vulpine grin—and goes back to hunting mice.

There are two seasons during which foxes are most likely to dine on grouse. One, of course, is the cold weather period of late winter when birds take refuge in fluffy snow. The other—and most success-

Red foxes prey on grouse throughout the year. PHOTO BY SCOTT–SWEDBERG

ful—is springtime when cock partridges announce their presence by drumming and, later, when hens brood precious eggs. Visit any known fox den in the the spring: around it you will find the pitiful remains of grouse. Often the springtime kill is measurably hiked because a biddy snatched off a clutch of eggs dooms that entire brood.

Gardiner Bump and his colleagues listed gray and red foxes first among nest violators, with weasels a close second, followed by skunks, raccoons, crows, and domestic dogs. It is unlikely that the smaller home-wreckers destroy many adult pats, yet all play havoc with eggs and immature birds.

Certainly foxes prowl grouse covers in every season; and despite all their natural cunning, superb noses and ears, they can be caught napping. Once, cruising a scrub oak plateau in mid-November, I focused on a motionless spot of orange against a gray background some hundred yards through the brush to my right front. Quite suddenly and surely I knew this to be a cherry red fox curled up on a boulder, dozing in the pale sunlight.

That day all the elements were on my side. A half gale was blowing from the fox to me, and the scrub oaks were noisy enough to swallow alien sound. Perhaps the wind, which had made pats spooky and kept me from decking a single bird, helped to incur sudden wrath, or maybe it was the thought of a prime pelt. Quickly I chambered a couple of high-based 2's, in place of the usual 8's, and then walked forward.

At approximately thirty yards some sound or instinct warned the fox and he seemed to explode out of deep sleep to make a looping, sidewise jump. The shot caught him in midair and he was as dead as any centered partridge before ever hitting the ground. That pelt is now on my study wall. Sometimes I gaze at it and then let my eyes wander to a collection of grouse tails. Big fish eat little fish, and who is the reiver?

On another day my brother Dick and I were hunting a side hill where birches marched down from a hardwood ridge. Junipers luxuriated there and barberries hung in clusters. We had moved a few pats, hardly the number expected, and then crows began to clamor in the valley below. Dick had a patent call in his vest pocket and, for want of something better to do, he sounded a rallying cry.

The black flyers weren't convinced, but a gray fox came slipping up through the birches and junipers. He *may* have been stalking crows himself, or he *may* have been dreaming about deer mice—but Dick suspected that we had a plausible reason for the day's scarcity of grouse: they'd been pushed right over the hill.

Among the chief grouse predators, and especially among those who specialize in the liquidation of adult birds, one must list the great horned owl. This silent pirate slaughters pats and is usually found in any area where birds are plentiful. Moreover, a minor southward migration of the species places more of them in upland covers during the late winter months when grouse are having all they can do to survive. Protected in many states, the great horned owl has demonstrated its predilection for pats by taking them right out of game-farm pens where experimental work is being conducted. No other native owl is so lethal an operator.

If I am hunting a state where the great horned owl is unprotected,

The great horned owl is a major winged predator of pats.

I will shoot each and every one that shows in upland cover. While no species should be exterminated, there is reason to protect the more valuable by controlling a known killer. I think it doubtful, in any event, that hunters could eliminate this tiger on wings, for it works its evils at night and largely remains hidden during the day. Therefore I have a bone to pick with do-gooders who have convinced legislatures that the great horned owl should be protected at all seasons. Ill-informed nature lovers are robbing Peter to pay Paul: the ruffed grouse suffers.

This very year, at the end of a bitter November day when partridges seemed nonexistent, I had gained the hard road just as full darkness descended. Away up in the pines to eastward there was the measured hooting of an owl. As if answering, and this was a full two months prior to any romantic nonsense, another sent the echoes pulsating out of a nearby cedar swamp.

It was too dark to stalk either bird, but I could visualize each of them—savage crown princes of the night, no longer sleepy and blinking in the harsh light of full day, but coming alive. Perched in the inscrutable black growth, ear-tufted heads swiveling, they would be probing the brush with wide yellow eyes and keen ears.

An owl's hoot is used to communicate with others of its kind, but the sound serves a far deadlier purpose. In the hushed woodlands that shout is a chilling prelude to murder. Having sent his fierce cry through the darkening hills and valleys, an owl attunes his remarkable ears to the slightest startled scraping of feet or the movement of a body. Any minute sound is enough to pinpoint a victim and, within scant seconds, the silent wings and extended claws are there.

True, that distinctive *hoo-hoo, hoo-hoo,* two long and two short notes (unless you're very close and can hear the initial first note of five syllables), is immeasurably wild and eerie in the hush of twilight, and the sound is as cold as death.

Some feel that snowy owls are quite as deadly as the great horned, but they are infrequent travelers south of Canada's Precambrian shield—and hardly a bird of the deep woods. In years when arctic buffers are scarce, the ghostly flyers move southward, taking all sorts of game. However, unlike the other big owls, snowies operate in full daylight and prefer wide open spaces, such as the seacoast and open fields: they certainly collect more ducks, rabbits, and ring-necked pheasants than grouse.

The goshawk, a contraction of "grouse hawk," is a deadly enemy of grouse in northern coverts. Fortunately, this hawk is rarely plentiful. PHOTO BY SCOTT–SWEDBERG

Barred owls harvest occasional pats, even though the greater part of their diet consists of small rodents. Even smaller night-flying hunters may strike down the odd bird. John Alden Knight, in *The Ruffed Grouse*, tells of an adult pat killed by a tiny screech owl. I think this unusual and hardly normal in the annals of predation. In fact, if we eliminate the great horned owl, our grouse would suffer little harm from the grasping claws of the silent marauders.

In north-central latitudes, goshawks regularly raid covers, and a goshawk is quite capable of catching a partridge in full flight. The big gray-blue accipiter of the north is an implacable enemy of grouse, and birds are patently terrified when one appears in native coverts. To escape, a pat will dive into a snowdrift, or even alight at the feet of a human being.

Goshawks are swift, strong, and utterly fearless. They will rocket through heavy cover in the wake of a bird and will even follow the quarry through a tangled brushpile or bank of blackberry brambles.

Inevitably hunters and goshawks make rather violent contact in northern coverts, and there are many tales of hawks shot down in the very act of killing grouse, both birds decked with a single charge. One year at Dover-Foxcroft, Maine, I came rather close.

Bob Williams and I were working the edge of a run-down apple orchard, hunting parallel, about fifty feet apart. Bob is, in the parlance of the Western story, a very fast gun, so some competition was involved. While I know that competition is not supposed to exist between hunters and fishers, let me tell you that this is a myth.

That day Williams and I had taken one pat together, practically demolishing the bird, and later I had my hands full to prevent him from stealing mine after two had flushed simultaneously, one to the right and one to the left. Swinging on my bird, I saw Bob dump his— and then turn toward mine. That time I beat him to the shot.

The memory was still fresh in my mind as a grouse came whipping over the birches with a goshawk right on its tail. This was a classic Station Eight shot, but I thought Williams would be challenging and I swung too fast. Probably the tail end of the pattern caught the pat, for it tumbled, and the hawk zoomed, unharmed. Curiously, I remained transfixed, never loosing a second charge. Bob was in thick cover and he saw none of this.

My Maine goshawk disappeared, a thing contrary to many instances of this kind. Often the bird is so intent on its prey that neither man nor pounding guns can drive it away. There are tales of these ardent raptors swooping back time and again, until they are tumbled by bird shot.

Again, motoring down out of Canada after a week of Atlantic salmon fishing in September, two of us saw a goshawk strike a grouse in midair. The pat came out of a stand of black growth, flying at full throttle. Right behind it, a big blue hawk accelerated and struck. There was a streaming puff of feathers and the two birds seemed to plummet earthward in one fluttering mass.

We were traveling at some seventy miles an hour, so the drama encompassed no more than a second. By the time I'd braked and backed a couple of hundred feet, neither bird was visible, although feathers still floated over the highway.

Only two other hawks are accomplished grouse killers, and both seem attracted to chicks or immatures. The Cooper's and sharp-shinned are successively smaller editions of the fierce northern goshawk—perhaps too small to handle an adult grouse with comfort, but quite capable of picking off chicks and half-grown birds.

Other hawks undoubtedly dine on pats, but I am sure that a majority of them are too slow, or too baffled by heavy cover to make any great inroads upon the species. A peregrine (duck hawk) is big enough and fast enough, but it simply does not haunt the tangled uplands. Many of the broad-winged breed, the red-shouldered, red-tailed, and marsh hawks may catch unwary grouse, but I would guess that these are targets of opportunity few and far between.

I am not fond of foxes, owls, and goshawks in my covers, but I respect these untamable corsairs of the fringe woodlands. No such emotion is extended to the house cat, a species that kills for the pure joy of killing. Fortunately, true wildcats are seldom very plentiful in partridge coverts close to civilization, but the domestic tabby more than makes up for this lack.

Among animals, a cat is the perfect killing machine, and an old feline roving the woodlots and slashings will destroy a surprising number of chicks and immatures. Many bring their prizes back home, more dead than alive, to torture and kill at leisure.

Aware of the fact that kittens become cats, too many questionably soft-hearted Americans dispose of unwanted litters by abandoning them on country roads. Those that survive without benefit of human-kind become game killers of note. Occasional feral toms attain tremendous size and, in so doing, slaughter a great variety of songbirds and game, including grouse. While chicks suffer the heaviest mortality, adult birds are sometimes taken.

Feral dogs kill game birds, yet there is little evidence of appreciable slaughter. Quite possibly the wildest of these animals, the cross called coydog by game biologists, may be as cunning as foxes or true coyotes: they are never plentiful and, usually, are blamed for more sin than they might rightly claim.

I recall a litter of "wild" dogs that several of us found in an abandoned cowshed on a long-forgotten farm. The adults were unapproachable and the pups were never tamed, although they were placed with responsible country families. In this instance we found ample evidence of wild fodder. There were the remains of cotton-tail rabbits, squirrels, and ring-necked pheasants, together with some domestic poultry—but there was no hint of ruffed grouse.

As a partridge killer the free-roving domestic dog seldom attains any high standard of efficiency. That they do harry birds is obvious. Tracks in the snow tell how dog after dog cruises coverts and follows grouse. Almost always this is a fruitless undertaking, for the end of the trail is a slash of primaries where the bird took wing long before the following dog was close enough to make an honest attempt at capture. The country dog certainly wrecks partridge nests, yet he ranks far down on any list of killers.

Of course coyotes, timber wolves, bobcats, and lynxes, in those areas where they coexist with grouse, are predators. Fortunately none are very abundant in the suburban covers frequented by most of our upland hunters. They are the reivers of the true wilderness, the remote lands rarely visited by humans. There a genuine balance is achieved and the end result is probably beneficial.

Close to humankind, smaller wild predators score great successes during the spring nesting season. That's when weasels, skunks, and raccoons delight in the discovery of nests and just-hatched chicks. The weasel is particularly deadly, ranking second only to the fox as a threat to young of the year. Red squirrels destroy eggs and will eat those well along in the process of incubation. Chipmunks and mice sometimes roll eggs out of a nest and—nobody seems to know why—bury them in nearby leaf mold. Pheasants sometimes deposit their eggs in grouse nests; then, when young ringnecks hatch early, the partridge biddy may desert her own clutch as hopeless.

The common crow is a springtime predator. Sharp-eyed and cunning, he'll locate a nest by watching the hen in her comings and goings, or by observing the human being who finds a clutch and must inspect it at frequent intervals. In the end of it, a well-briefed crow may steal and puncture every egg.

There are so many villains eager to undo a broody grouse's handiwork! In Mason-Dixon country, opossums delight in the discovery of eggs. Razorback hogs appreciate wild omelets. Blacksnakes and rattlesnakes have been accused, but the former finds an abundance of forage during the short period when grouse are nesting, and the latter is never very plentiful in grouse coverts.

Cattle, sheep, and goats seldom are listed among grouse killers, yet all may contribute to the decline of partridges. They do so by denuding ground cover. While one finds grouse nonchalantly feeding within yards of dairy cows, grazing animals and pats are never compatible where the grazers are hard pressed for forage. Cattle destroy understory, and a grouse must have sufficient ground cover to complete its life cycle. There is no problem until such time as too many cattle, sheep, or goats are pastured on a given acreage. Then an upland cover is cropped clean and resident pats retire to the next hill.

Normal grazing may be beneficial in some coverts particularly where pole timber has succeeded in pushing grouse back, or where dense woodland has choked off understory. In this case a hunter may find many pats in rough pastureland. When a proper balance is achieved, game prospers.

Grazing actually benefits woodcock, a game bird often taken by grouse hunters in the eastern half of the country. Timberdoodles delight in muddy pastures, so hunters work such areas with woodcock in mind and the occasional grouse as a bonus. In summary, light grazing is a boon, while overexploitation drives pats back into the boondocks.

Similarly, in areas where deer have multiplied to a saturation point, usually through sanctuary or ill-advised buck laws that ensure a proliferation of small does, ground cover is devoured. Before the deer themselves begin to die of starvation in wintertime, the browse line creeps above a man's shoulder height.

While adult partridges can subsist on a great variety of foods, taken at all levels, the effect of overgrazing is apparent on springtime broods. Grouse chicks must have brushy clearings in order to survive. For them a clean, parklike woodland is a biological desert. One cannot fault the husbandman whose stock has first call on private lands, but there are sulfurous things to be said about conservation commissioners who allow deer to become too plentiful for their own good. Too many hooves and nibbling jaws can be as deadly as a scourge of predators.

Major predators, thankfully, seldom occur in great numbers. They proliferate when buffers are plentiful; hence, peak rabbit years will see a corresponding peak in wildcats, owls, and foxes. A sudden population explosion of any small rodent triggers a new abundance of killers—and these turn to grouse as targets of opportunity when the buffers begin to disappear.

There are too many "ifs" and "buts" in this picture for anyone to draw definitive lines. For example, it is the easiest thing in this blue-eyed world to credit a shortage of any species, say grouse, to an inordinate increase in predators, such as foxes, owls or—you name it.

Nobody really knows the precise interrelationship of buffer populations and predation, let alone the facts about such seconding buffers as grouse in an abnormal situation where the usual food species have been thinned out and the killers are scratching for survival.

Logic is roadblocked by a great variety of arguments. Skunks, for example, delight in rustling partridge eggs from a nest, but the woods pussy is a farm-suburban animal, rarely plentiful in the hinterlands. Goshawks have been called "partridge hawks" for good reason, yet they are a northern to north-central species and rarely venture very far into the southernmost range of the grouse. We have local population explosions of the various predators, usually prompted by preceding booms in buffers.

Then, of course, it is wise to note that certain killers are more active, or at least more lethal, during specific seasons. Foxes, weasels, house cats, skunks, raccoons and domestic dogs, together with a host of predatory birds and smaller animals, are most annoying to pats in springtime. Cooper's and sharp-shinned hawks, together with foxes, fare well in early summer when chicks and immatures offer easy targets. Throughout late fall and winter the great horned owl, aided by foxes, takes a toll. How much? Some say half the spring brood, but no one really knows.

Moreover, the demands of latitude, terrain, and availability of buffers act on predators as well as quarry. There may be instances in which a certain killer has enjoyed a population explosion, and then control may be desirable—but it should be control based on documented fact, not emotion.

The average hunter, because he has so few facts upon which to base an educated guess, usually is unable to arrive at any deliberate, cool, and uncompromising decision. When he acts, as I did in shooting the red fox off his warm boulder, he is the victim of emotion. Perhaps I am wrong in my dislike of the great horned owl as a co-frequenter of grouse coverts. Certainly game biologists tell us that predator control, widely practiced, has yet to prove a key to the protection or increase of grouse.

Therefore, it would be presumptuous of me to suggest operational procedures when you meet any of the known grouse killers in your favorite coverts. It is necessary to recall again that many states protect certain predators. Surely the marauders serve a useful purpose, and honesty dictates an admission that many of them are blamed for more crime than they commit. Control is a very delicate operation.

Finally, chew over one basic fact: Man is the ultimate predator and his deadliest weapons are pollution, the bulldozer, the layer of cement that extinguishes all things green and growing. Automobiles take a horrendous number of birds. No year passes in which I do not find scores of grouse either ground into the pavement or crumpled in the gutters of suburban highways. Clutches of chicks, together with the biddy, often succumb to speeding motor cars. The very fact that this proud game bird goes its own way, scorning the hurtling masses of metal that scream over American highways and byways, ensures a murderous casualty rate.

The gun is a minor reiver.

Hen grouse and half-grown chick killed by a motorcar in June.

THREE • THE BUCCANEERS

*I*n any discussion of the grouse in America, conversation must sooner or later swing around to market hunters and their impact on the partridges of a golden age. Today's sportsmen generally are convinced that the kill-for-cash gunner was a buccaneer of the uplands, a primary factor in the more or less continuous decline of bird populations during the past hundred years.

I suppose it would be spectacular to expose a generation of game hogs. Indeed some ill-informed citizens, together with a few who perpetuate misinformation as a lever for anti-gun legislation, still insist that the market hunter was a despicable character who exterminated game. The evidence is contrary.

Quite naturally, those of us who delight in today's upland shooting want to know more about these old titans of the scatter-gun. What equipment served them before the advent of modern, controlled loads? Were they pot-shooters who cared little for the game they bagged, or enthusiasts who took a keen delight in sport? Crack shots—or duffers who scored because the birds were both tame and plentiful?

The literature of American gunning provides answers, up to a point, but too often the facts are stripped of emotion. Sadly, all skeletal histories offer data that can be variously interpreted. Fortunately, in my youth, I met a few patriarchs who had killed grouse for the market and I made it my business to interrogate them before they hunted around the bend and disappeared into the rosy fog of legend.

I remember Fred Bucklin of Brookfield, Massachusetts, conceded by his peers to have been one of the greatest wing shots of a highly professional era. Then there was Bill "Hound Dog" Deviou, another notable market hunter, and Everett St. John, a wonderful old conservationist who had sold one grouse in his youth and therefore maintained tongue-in-cheek kinship with the kill-for-cash group of the nineties. Deviou and St. John lived in Worcester, Massachusetts, a city located in the center of a state that witnessed intense market-hunting activity.

Singly, and yet with surprising concurrence on important issues, these men told the story of a colorful era, listed the great shots of their time, and offered opinions about the decline in grouse populations. They had some mighty farfetched hypotheses and, like old men in any time slot, they were somewhat disparaging of youth, terribly opinionated, and possessed of a view-with-alarm syndrome. None believed that market shooting played an important part in the decline of partridges, and I am inclined to agree with them.

Central Massachusetts was, and is, magnificent grouse country. Forgive me if I dwell on the exploits of these Bay State sharpshooters for a few paragraphs. This Yankeeland happens to be the place where it all started, and it is also the place where I met my first market hunters. Actually, these specialists were prototypes of gunners found throughout the nation at that time; they were not peculiar to the Northeast.

In the beginning of it all, when the Pilgrims waded ashore, birds were concentrated in the edges, along the river bottoms and in the brushy rims of clearings. Never in history were they very plentiful in the deep, aboriginal woodlands, nor are they now.

During the late 1600s passenger pigeons and heath hens were more important than grouse as a marketable resource. Throughout the first two hundred years of settlement pigeons darkened the skies during their spring and fall migrations. Heath hens abounded on flatlands close to the seaboard. Both species were netted, shot, and even clubbed in astronomical numbers. While grouse flourished in the river bottoms and at the edge of timber, they were more difficult to harvest in appreciable numbers, and so they were not exploited.

Of course *some* partridges were always being snared, shot, and sold on the open market, together with pigeons and heath hens—and *some* farsighted individuals came to decry the practice. As early as 1832 the sale of game birds was attacked in Massachusetts. To no avail, naturally, for New Englanders were generally agreed that game belonged to the countryman. Deer, waterfowl, pigeons, heath hens, grouse, and woodcock represented a cash crop. Those who were fitted by training and temperament to reap the annual harvest were honored

An old photo of one of the last heath hens in Massachusetts. The species is now extinct.

in their community. Pigeon nets still rot under the eaves of Yankee farmhouses, and many a fowling piece that once took its grim toll of birds now graces a reconstructed colonial mantelpiece.

Passenger pigeons and heath hens began to disappear prior to the Civil War. Land use and overexploitation finally exterminated both, leaving the ruffed grouse and the woodcock as the only fair game for commercial flesh hunters. Thereafter, when prices were high enough to warrant the expenditure of powder and shot, occasional village ne'er-do-wells spent their waking hours killing pats and 'doodles with everything from muzzle-loading shotguns to the running noose.

Snares were set on drumming logs and in the runs frequented by birds. Professionals sometimes manufactured "runs" by building sylvan brush fences with convenient openings in which nooses were positioned. In wintertime, paths were swept in the snow and snares rigged where they'd accomplish greatest slaughter. This was a trick learned from the Indians.

In those early days, according to literature and legend, countrymen employed "bark dogs," curs of uncertain origin used to tree grouse and to keep them occupied until a gunner could arrive and knock off x number of birds, lowest first, and so on. The ruffed grouse of near antiquity must have been extraordinarily trusting, although some accounts would seem to dispute the fact. Audubon, for example, later found it impossible to work the trick, and he thought it a folk legend.

New England's first citizens were farmers. They cleared land and moved slowly westward as the stubborn climate and the equally stubborn Indians permitted. These Yankees were thrifty: good land use to them meant clean pastures, massive stone walls to corral their stock, and northern orchards set to apples. Villages mushroomed, each with its spired church. Lumbermen denuded surrounding forests, and husbandmen moved in. Grouse moved back to the edges.

All of this happened, mind you, before Abe Lincoln was a toddler. New England was a thriving community when the West was still a vast white beckoning nothingness on a map. The settlers conquered their wilderness and straightway endeavored to slaughter available game. They did this with every means at hand but, although no one recognized as much, land use was a major weapon.

Here, as in the Adirondacks, birds were plentiful when early farms were operated as going concerns. Sometimes, in fact, pats were too cussed abundant for the taste of landsmen who called for bounties on birds that insisted upon budding precious apple trees. There is no reason to doubt, though, that clean farming pushed grouse back to the rough perimeter of each homestead. Orchards and gardens offered no protective cover, so birds prospered in nearby woodlots and slashings.

Then, as so often happens in the history of a new country, settlers began to move out—and the wilderness crept back. New Englanders left their tidy farms and rocky pastures. They went West, dreaming of deeper topsoil and land grants; they followed the gold rushes or they sought easy money in the burgeoning industry of big cities. Finally the Civil War disrupted family dynasties and thousands of sidehill farms were deserted. The patient brush sprang up, almost hiding old, huddled apple trees. Stone walls heaved with winter frosts.

Wild grapes and bittersweet climbed over the gray stones. Grouse proliferated.

Since New England was an old land before most of America was seen by white men, the market hunters of the late 1800s, regarded as ancients by modern sportsmen, were actually ranging cover that had been deserted by civilization before *they* were born. The pioneer's back forty and woodlot, his pasture and orchard had sprouted brush. Even the cellar holes of early settlers were hosting tall paper birches, and the lilacs were lost in a wilderness. Today, in the stone-wall country of New England, antiquarians probe depressions where towering hardwoods shade arbutus, searching for artifacts of a civilization that seems as remote and legendary as lost Atlantis.

In the late 1800s, few regarded this exodus as anything unusual. Grouse, always ready to reclaim a territory, were back in tremendous numbers. For them, this reseeding was manna from heaven. For a wonderful period they enjoyed sufficient light cover and water, dusting slopes, conifers for shelter and an abundance of food produced by the sunbathed brush. Partridges multiplied and market hunting reached its zenith in those years that followed the end of the Civil War and the first decade of a stern new century.

Actually, market hunting is another of those trick phrases, since it implies that all birds peddled to the flesh marts were taken with firearms. In fact, a great share of the early kill was made by trappers who employed snares and who were too thrifty to waste a charge of powder and shot on any partridge. All through the seventeenth, eighteenth, and nineteenth centuries, country boys set horsehair nooses to catch grouse. After the Civil War, when a ready market developed for these birds, wire snares became more popular—and these are still used by a scattering of poachers.

Records kept by thrifty farmers and merchants in the market-hunting days indicate that prices rose and fell with the seasonal abundance of game, ranging from as little as eight cents apiece to a high of ten dollars a brace after no-sale laws had been passed and bootlegging (birdlegging?) became popular. Probably twenty-five to seventy-five cents a bird was near average during the heyday of shooting.

In this connection it should be noted that honest shooters never made any amount of folding money. Illicit profits were enjoyed by those who continued to operate after legislatures had banned the sale of birds early in the twentieth century. This was a period in which the market hunter became a whipping boy for all manner of ills besetting game. It never occurred to the multitudes that land use might be a greater limiting factor than any number of guns and snares.

About 1870, after the passenger pigeon had been pushed toward extinction and the heath hen was not far from the same fate, the legendary market hunter of our prehistory was born. This was a new breed of sportsman, and I use the word deliberately: he was a transition between the ancient reaper of the land's largess and the modern outdoorsman.

Suddenly it became immoral to kill a grouse with a snare. Those market shooters who operated through the late 1800s and the first decade of the twentieth century despised contemporaries who employed the running noose. Moreover, they ignored the questionable bark dog, introduced pointing breeds, and insisted upon shooting grouse in flight.

Modern gunners may question this conclusion, and there is no doubt that a certain percentage of the old-timers coveted a heavy bag and were not concerned about sport. The great ones *were* concerned, and I quote parts of two letters I received immediately after the death of Fred Bucklin in 1962.

An old gentleman, obviously a contemporary of Fred's, wrote: "I saw the account of Fred Bucklin's death in the *Worcester Telegram* and wondered if it was the same Fred Bucklin that I knew, and you were kind enough to straighten me out. He was nine years older than myself. While telling about market hunters you failed to mention Jay Snell. While hunting with him I saw him shoot a partridge on the ground. That sickened me of him. . . ."

In all fairness to the late Jay Snell, who was indeed a great market hunter in central Massachusetts, his kill-for-cash days ended when the law prohibited any sale of birds. Snell thereupon became a game warden and served with great distinction.

Mrs. Clare Bucklin LaFountain, daughter of the famous market hunter, also wrote to me. She said, in part:

"I wish to express my deep appreciation for your fine story about Frederick Bucklin, my father. I had thought there was no one left who remembered those days, and it does my heart good to learn that this is not so.

"A good deal of it happened before my time, but I remember the clear, cold autumn mornings, with a sprinkle of frost on the ground, when George Chapin of Brookfield used to come down, sometimes with Jay Clark of Worcester or 'Em,' Herbert Emery, to go hunting with my father back in the '20s.

"George used to say: 'We would get all the guns, cartridges, dogs and lunches in the car, ready to go—and then Fred would have to light his pipe.' That was a ritual which must precede any significant event. There was excitement in the air, and somehow it was accentuated by the lighting of the pipe.

"When they came home at night with partridges and woodcock, my father used to lay his birds on the table and say: 'Well, I got two partridges and two woodcock,' or whatever it was, 'but I don't know as I get much satisfaction out of it. To tell the truth, I wish I could put them back in the trees the way they were this morning!'

"There is the apparent inconsistency of hunters! Most of them love bird and animals, and yet they shoot them. However, these two attitudes are no less reconcilable than the general inconsistencies of human nature, and each of them is valid—neither cancels out the other. The keen enjoyment of the hunter, pitting his wit and marksmanship against the quarry's native sagacity and speed, contrasted with later regret that something has been killed are simply human moods of different tone."

So—as I have always suspected—Bucklin and the other great market hunters felt much as we do in this atomic age. He loved the hunt beyond all human endeavors, and yet there was a measure of sadness when he held a downed biddy in his hand and stroked its immaculate feathers.

"I wish I could put them back in the trees the way they were this morning!"

The late 1800s was a time of change, and our gunners had the best of intentions. They sold birds, because this was customary, but they set new standards and began to think of the future. In this connection it is well to recall that English gentlemen still sell the red grouse they kill on well-managed moors. In itself, sale is no sin. Tragedy lies only in the rape of a renewable resource.

Prior to the no-sale ban, which became effective in Massachusetts in 1900, market shooters were a class unto themselves. Neighbors re-

A typical turn-of-the-century bag of grouse, with a few woodcock mixed in. The photo was made from an old stained-glass negative. The gunner is Charley Faux of Worcester; he and his partner, Arthur Burns, collected this bag in one and one half days, traveling by horse-drawn trap.

63

garded them as "great hunters," and they were respected. Some attained near-hero status and are still recalled in the sleepy little towns of central New England.

In those days, and I am now referring to the late 1800s, a partridge hunter deserted his plow or forge on September first. For approximately four months he worked the uplands with gun and dog, shooting grouse and woodcock for city gourmets. The grouse, and bags of five to ten a day were nearer average than the well-remembered twenty-five and thirty, were sent "down t'Boston" where they brought anywhere from 50¢ to $1.50 a brace. Local fanciers sometimes paid one dollar each.

Fred Bucklin, who was eighty-three years old when I interviewed him in 1947, told me that 350 birds a man was a fine season's bag. Since Fred, by all accounts, was one of the best of a highly select group, his summation should have been accurate.

Such shooting was not confined to Massachusetts. Everywhere in the range of grouse, hinterlanders harvested the available resource. Packed into barrels or boxed for shipment, the birds came bouncing into New York and Philadelphia and Washington, D.C. They were sold in Chicago and Cincinnati and in the big towns of Michigan. Birds from Maine and Canada often graced the menus of the great hotels.

Yet, curiously, the marksman who could knock off 350 pats in a season was not thereby made wealthy. He had to feed himself and his dogs, purchase guns, ammunition, and ancillary gear. He had to travel from cover to cover, usually via rail or horse-drawn trap. Professional market hunters spent the days shooting and the nights playing cards. "It was hard work," Bucklin recalled, "but, Lord, what sport!" The dogs, he told me, were brier-torn and footsore. "Many a Gordon setter wore home-made boots to keep his pads from bleeding."

Since these hardworking market hunters reached their coverts by rail, buckboard—or often via shank's mare—their sphere of operations was necessarily limited. Probably some of the better grouse range, because of its very inaccessibility, remained virgin for decades.

December was considered a top month for gunning, since cold weather made the birds lie close—another testimonial to the fact that our partridge has always been difficult to approach. But, whether the temperature soared to eighty degrees in September, or dropped to zero after Thanksgiving, hunters went afield. They were out there when spider webs still glittered in the early fall and birch aphids made life a ticklish misery, and they were there when snow sifted through the hardwoods.

Again, the ancient question: Were these old-timers motivated by greed or enthusiasm? A little of both, perhaps, but there is no doubt that sport came first. "We gave away as many as we sold," Deviou grinned, "and I remember a winter when the family lived on partridge breasts."

The profit motive must be eliminated from consideration. "We used it as an excuse," Bucklin chuckled. "No hunter ever made a nickel on birds, but we had a lot of fun." Obviously these were sportsmen, proud of their skill, able to take a four-month vacation in the field without risking bankruptcy, and marketing some of their birds for a pittance. At least the grouse weren't wasted.

Immediately following the no-sale ban, prices soared to as much as five dollars a bird. "That law was the worst thing that ever happened to pa'tridge," Bucklin growled, "because it made bootlegging profitable. The market price went sky high and practically everybody disregarded the law. It was like prohibition."

The ban's immediate effect was to ensure more shooting pressure on an already dwindling bird population. In addition to the temptation of easy money, everybody wanted to get into the act. People who had never fired a shotgun at grouse purchased weapons and headed for the nearest coverts. They accomplished no great slaughter, but they killed birds through sheer force of numbers.

Market hunting was now teetering on the brink of oblivion, but there was no hint of this during the first decade of a new century. The old scofflaws reveled in high prices, and the new legions of amateurs dreamed of riches. It took a succession of low points in grouse population, plus better law enforcement and education, to choke off demand and to frighten an increasing number of genuine sportsmen. Gradually all shooters—including the deadly market hunters of the late 1800s—became convinced that the bird they loved needed protection.

Many of the famous professionals became the staunchest of conservationists when protective laws were passed. Some earned their livelihood in later years as game wardens. All had personal theories about cycles of scarcity and abundance. Bucklin, for example, was sure that the partridges of New England declined when blight claimed that region's majestic chestnut trees. He thought that the chestnut boasted a tannic acid required by the bird.

Henry A. Mower, another great shooter of this era, was convinced that the introduction of ring-necked pheasants sounded a death rattle for pats. It was his firm belief that the imported Asiatic chased partridges out of their native coverts and would kill the American bird on sight. Though he was wrong, primarily because grouse and pheasants choose different types of cover, it is interesting to note that ring-necks sometimes injure pats by laying their eggs in the nests of the native species.

Everett St. John always declared that land use was the dominant factor. Everett lived long enough to see modern game management in action, and until the day of his death at eighty-six he was sharp enough to insist that grouse always return to deserted farmlands where cover assures food and protection.

Today's sportsmen have every right to inquire about the skills of these so-called great hunters. All evidence indicates that they were

The late Everett St. John of Worcester, Massachusetts, who sold one grouse in his youth and therefore claimed kinship with the old kill-for-cash gunners. St. John became an ardent conservationist. Here, in his early eighties, he weighs grouse for the benefit of research.

infernally accurate. Bucklin, it was said, could toss five empty shells into the air and hit each with a charge of bird shot before any touched the ground. The old-timers admitted that this might be a trick, but they swore that Fred was quite as deadly in the uplands, with live targets scrambling over the birch tops. Considering the crotchety nature of old men who have been champions in their day, it is significant to note that all rated Bucklin either superior or equal.

Bill "Hound Dog" Deviou, seventy-seven when I met him in 1947, had spent one day afield during that season. He was an old man, and apparently frail, yet he announced: "I seen two pa'tridges and killed 'em both. They get mighty seasick when I p'int the old Winchester."

Everett St. John, right up until the year of his death, went afield when the red maples flamed. Toward the end of his life, he worked with wildlife management personnel in the collecting of grouse wings and tails. Every biddy he shot was carefully weighed, measured, and sexed—and young technicians found that he knew his business. Everett was a crack shot, even though in old age his eyes were dimming and he could spend no more than an hour at a time in the uplands.

These old boys were fabulous marksmen, and it is no good to say that birds, in their era, laid close to the gun and provided so many easy opportunities. They were accurate because they had more time to practice, even with firearms that, by today's standards, would be considered antique. They made the best of their limited ordnance. I often wonder, if the years could be rolled back and a competition arranged, whether any one of us could stay with them in the fields of woodcraft or shooting. I'd have to bet against us!

In the late 1800s a man like Fred Bucklin could, and often did, kill twenty-five birds in a single day (not counting woodcock). Breech-loading shotguns had arrived, and every partridge hunter had his own loading formula. Clayt Adams of Oakham, Massachusetts, one of the all-time greats, used five drams of black powder behind one and one-half ounces of number 11 or 12 shot in his 10-gauge double. This might be exceeded today, but it was big poison in its time.

Most of the aces favored doubles in 10 and 12 gauge, with tubes sawed off to 24 or 25 inches in an effort to spread the pattern. Some went so far as to bell the muzzles. They liked big open bores and small shot. After the leaves had fallen and woodlands were relatively open, some of these specialists would load with 9's, but this was pretty close to maximum. Nobody used the currently popular 7½'s.

There is another bit of history that intrigues me, particularly in view of the present delusion that no weapon other than a side-by-side double is really adequate on grouse. Market hunters used doubles until repeating shotguns became available: then, almost to a man, they switched. Winchester's sweet-pointing Model 1897 was a great favorite. This was the weapon that ended an era, and it was considered the deadliest of all scatter-guns during the last gasp years of kill-for-cash.

Few sharpshooters of the nineties preached the virtues of 16 gauge, for this was still an "odd" English boring, destined to become extremely popular in the 1920s and '30s, and then to slide back into near obscurity. The 20 was unknown, and old-timers would have sneered at its proportions.

Early American market hunters killed pats with muzzleloaders like this nicely engraved English Onion & Wheelock.

Guns of the day were heavy, but countrymen who were used to hard labor during the eight months or so in which they scrabbled for sustenance thought nothing of carrying a bulky firearm from dawn to dusk. On the other hand, they had an eye for beauty in their weapons. Top shooters took pride in custom guns, handsomely engraved, inlaid with precious metals and stocked with selected walnut. Few appreciated a pistol grip on a shotgun.

There is little doubt that birds were easy to find in the good years, but it wasn't all wine and roses. Periodic shortages of grouse have been recorded ever since the Pilgrims landed in New England, and undoubtedly the Indians had noted the same curious fluctuations for thousands of years prior to this. Back in 1882, partridges were so

The gun that ended an era. American market hunters deserted double-barreled shotguns when Winchester unveiled its classic Model 1897 cornsheller. This repeater was favored by professionals in the last-gasp years of market hunting.

scarce in central Massachusetts that Milt Allen, a great hunter of the time, gunned hard to get one bird. His objective: to have it mounted as a memento of the good old days!

Modern shooters like to alibi their failures by stating that pats of the golden era would lie closer to a dog. Maybe. But Henry William Herbert, who, under the pseudonym of Frank Forester, was America's foremost hunting and fishing journalist in the mid-1800s, sang a different tune. "They are the most trying bird to the temper of a dog that possibly can be imagined, as it is comparatively speaking of a very rare occurrence that they will lie to be pointed and flushed over the point."

Forester was not alone. In spite of rococo literature prepared by men who had no real rapport with the fringe wilderness, pioneering on-the-spot reports from Virginia to New England mention a wary and sagacious bird, hard to approach, difficult for a dog to pin, and rarely an easy target for the gunner.

I think that the great market hunters scored because they were crack wing shots and because they employed strains of pointers and setters that have vanished with their masters. The bloodlines have been lost, probably forever.

Perhaps it is unfair to dwell upon "strains" of pointers and setters. Today's strains may be quite as good, or even better. The atomic age dog lacks an opportunity to work great numbers of grouse and hone its natural skills to a fine edge. Since breeding generally improves, this is a charitable view. Still, the types of dogs favored by market hunters have few living counterparts.

They were big, slow animals—Gordon, English, and Irish setters. Toward the end of that flamboyant period of American grouse hunting, pointers became popular. Gordon setters were highly intelligent and affectionate, but they tended to be one-man dogs, suspicious of strangers and often savage with anyone but their masters. The big red Irish dogs were wild, but deadly under the hand of a hard-hunting and determined man. While Gordons were favored, many came to consider the English setter and pointer most tractable.

All the pointing breeds had one thing in common—the ability to work grouse and to point at maximum range. By today's standards, they were very slow. They worked head up, but they were sure. Since every man's choice in a true game bird was the ruffed grouse, no ring-necked pheasant upset the delicate psyche of a dog bred to work carefully and to point his quarry (unless it happened to be a plebeian woodcock) well out in thick cover. No southern pointer or setter, built like a whippet to race over flatlands for quail, had yet been seen in Yankee stone-wall coverts: these arrived on the scene much later, after the great grouse dogs of the nineties had passed to their Elysian runs.

I suppose we shall never know how good they really were, for dogs and men are long gone. They are the stuff of legend, and legend always prospers with the speeding years.

But history is a living thing. So those of us who love ruffed grouse and who insist upon poking our noses into the past have learned that the market hunter was no criminal: he was simply a sportsman who happened to arrive on center stage at a precise moment when upland shooting had reached a peak and a crossroads in America. He was a man like you and me, a partridge hunter who was very close to paradise when he caught a wily woods grouse in the center of a bird-shot pattern.

*E*very addicted grouse hunter is a contradiction in terms. He loves a great bird—and longs for a short open season in which he may legally kill it. The climactic moment in which a shot string intercepts a flying pat is etched in memory, yet throughout most of the year our upland gunner is this world's most zealous protector of ruffed grouse.

October and November are magic months. But harvesttime is an infinitesimal part of the whole. A grouse hunter is truly a man for all seasons: he is afield during every month of the year, and each month provides new information about the greatest game bird that has ever taken wing in our New World.

Literature on partridge hunting generally stems from the Northeast, and this is a pity since the bird's range is wide. A gunner might travel from Canada's Maritime Provinces down to northwest Georgia, and thence across our vast land to California, even into the Yukon Valley of Alaska—with side trips along the way—and find little difference in ruffed grouse. With few exceptions, where cover is adequate, these birds offer a sharp challenge to the fastest and most accurate of marksmen.

Such exceptions are now limited to remote areas in the far northern states and Canada. There, where black growth crowds in and ravens creak overhead, a pat may seem surprisingly tame and loath to fly. As elsewhere in its range, this curiously docile northern bird is taken at the edges and in brushy clearings. Its reluctance to flush may be the result of little contact with gun-bearing men, or perhaps there is something in the theory advanced by Dr. Malcolm K. Johnston of Boston, Massachusetts.

Dr. Johnston, as ardent a grouse hunter as he is a salt-water angler, wonders whether the "fool hen" pat of the North may not be the end result of a predation pattern. Away up in the cool spruces and hemlocks of Canada, according to this hypothesis, aerial raptors are more abundant than terrestrial predators. Goshawks and great horned owls outnumber foxes and other perils of the ground. Therefore the far northern grouse uses its wings only as a last resort, and then executes very short flights.

This is an interesting and debatable idea. Perhaps I have been hasty in dismissing the various subspecies as nit-picking by taxonomists. Maybe *Bonasa umbellus thayerie* of the eastern Maritimes, and *togata* of central Canada, are never so instinctively wild and wary as the much-hunted red ruff and gray ghost (*umbellus umbellus*) of the north-central regions in the United States. As biologists so often declare when they are stymied and need a stiff drink: further study is indicated.

Quite naturally, cover varies because of land conformation, climate, and flora. Principal forage depends on whatever is available in any given area, but because the partridge is so catholic in its tastes, this fact is of minor importance. Grouse gorge themselves on a variety of choice foods during any season of abundance, then make do with less-favored victuals during a regional hunger moon. The birds are highly adaptable, and any man who desires to study their habits must also study the land and its largess.

In this age of affluence and rapid transportation, an adventurous gunner might well inspect a variety of coverts during the course of a single week. He could sample pats feeding on Cape Cod cranberries at the edges of scrub pine barrens, or move inland to see the same bird feasting on fox grapes, acorns, and wild apples; fly to the haw berry and laurel thickets of the Appalachians or to the river bottoms of the Northern Rockies.

Grouse populate much of the southern Canadian and north-central American landmass. There has been a retreat in some central states of the United States because of land use, and quite naturally these birds do not frequent the deserts and great plains. Still, the biddy of the Maritimes is closely allied to the partridge of Michigan's Upper Peninsula, the popple-guarded river bottoms of British Columbia's Rocky Mountains, and the sunny clearings that etch the shadows of California's giant redwoods. The ruffed grouse, challenging ptarmigan in the streamside brush of Alaska's Yukon River country, are nearly identical to those a sportsman finds in New York's wonderful Adirondacks.

Upon hearing that a grouse-hunting book was on the way, Charles F. Waterman of DeLand, Florida, a fine outdoor writer and all-around sportsman, promptly offered sage observations on partridge coverts and tactics in Montana and British Columbia, areas with which I am not familiar. Waterman feels that "the best ruffed grouse shooting in the world must be in western Canada. It isn't easy shooting, but there are lots of birds and you do have a chance every now and then."

Charley thinks that "best" means an abundance of pats—here called willow grouse. It *is* likely, he admits, that British Columbia birds will alight in a conifer and refuse to fly, but there are so many of them that a gunner may choose his shots—including the tough ones that smash off through the brush.

Canadian-Pacific grouse are not plagued by heavy shooting pressure. Most of them fall to .22-caliber rifles or 410-gauge shotguns and

Charles F. Waterman collects a grouse in Montana. PHOTO BY CHARLES F. WATERMAN

Hunting the moist, well-foliaged coverts of Hazelton, British Columbia.
PHOTO BY CHARLES F. WATERMAN

they are sniped out of trees to provide camp meat. The enthusiast who prefers wing shooting enjoys many opportunities, and cover is varied. The climate is moist, to say the least. Much of the time you will have to wear foul-weather gear.

British Columbia birds are much easier to bag than those in Montana, where Waterman generally found them in very thick willows "and other stuff" along creeks and in canyons. When flushed, Montana's willow grouse tend to go into big conifers where you can't see them or drive them out. Most of the shooting occurs on a second flush. The dog points and the bird hops up a few feet out of reach. You hear wings beat and walk over there. When the pat flies you may have a chance for a snap shot.

Exceptions occur when grouse leave tangled creek beds to feed on juniper berries on nearby steep hillsides. Then a dog may hold them. Again, gunning may be in or along open forest edges. Charley recalls good sport with early fall birds along the edges, their crops full of grasshoppers—unusual in that adult pats have been touted as vegetarians.

When Rocky Mountain grouse are in thick cover they become difficult targets. Waterman speaks of hearing as many as six flushes without ever seeing a bird. I have advised him to "join the club." Identical complaints are registered by gunners wherever the pat reigns supreme.

Terrain varies and foodstuffs change, both with latitude and season, but basics remain. Enthusiastic shooters may seem blasé in the magnificence of mountain vistas and flaming sunsets—because they are concentrating on nearby aspen runs, birch-clad slopes, and apple trees planted by forgotten farmers. "Birdy looking," they mutter, and conspire to return with a light scatter-gun when shooting gets under way.

Primarily, any ruffed grouse requires food, water, and cover. Sunny edges and knolls are very important. There must be something in the way of winter sanctuary, whether it be the pines, junipers, and spruces of the north or the laurel and rhododendrons of the central and southern range. Partridges demand brushy clearings where broods can forage on warm spring days. Never look for this ultimate creation in open country, for it is a spirit of fringe woodlands, mountain benches, and river bottoms—always the rough, rugged territory that challenges mankind, or the land that has reverted to fringe wilderness after mankind, for one reason or another, has retreated.

Seasons will determine where grouse will be found in any area, but a covert of note is always a crazy quilt of environmental habitat. The partridge that stains his dainty beak with low-bush blackberries on an overgrown sidehill pasture in August will be seeking acorns and beechnuts in November. He will hasten to the laurel jungles or the sighing conifers when wintry weather grips the land, and he will then spend much time budding aspen and apple and birch, depending on availability.

When spring returns to any north-central covert, partridges lust after green tender shoots. They prospect the sunny edges and knolls, delouse themselves in dry flurries of dust—and salute the vernal equinox with much ecstatic drumming. It is a time for man to hunt, but not to kill. After a winter that seems endless, it is a triumphant thing to see a mourning cloak butterfly challenging the frost, to watch a deer go rocking off through bare hardwoods and, finally, to jump a brace of grouse out of the sear jungle of brush on a southwest slope. The event makes conversation for gunners who meet at lunchtime in great cities across America.

November woodlands in Ohio. PHOTO BY ERWIN A. BAUER

"Lots of birds around. Great brood year if it stays dry."

"I'll check Jackpot and The Sugarhouse next Saturday. Lord, we might even have another good year!"

Grouse hunters are optimists, and they enjoy prospecting quite as much—well, almost as much—as actual shooting. The hot spots are coded, and there is no key, since partners keep their own counsel.

Every partridge-hunting addict in this world of gunning has a few coverts that are his very own, not in deed and legal writ, of course, but because he has hunted them for years and knows the exact location of scattered junipers and sunny rimmings, each dappled knoll and dwarfed wild apple tree. If curses really withered right arms, the developers who frequently bulldoze such heavenly corners into new house lots would be in tough shape.

There is a delightful sense of cloak-and-dagger intrigue in the secretiveness with which old hands guard favored grounds. One simply does not speak of Asa Brown's back forty, or the laurel slope between

Route 1 and Seawrack Road. Each well-remembered bonanza, like the lost gold mines of the Rockies, flaunts a nickname suggested by some natural terrain feature, a glorious adventure, or a work of man. Thus we have corners known by such fanciful and pithy titles as The Rich Widow, Dead Horse, Sally's Backhouse, Bowel Movement, and Straw Hollow. Every partridge shooter can add place names, few of which are so designated on government topo maps.

A covert is a treasure, and he who shares his riches with another must be considered a true friend. There are men who would more willingly share their wives—although I suppose this is logical, considering that wives aren't plagued by cycles of abundance and decline and can even be replaced in the event of a poor season.

Inevitably, the partridge hunter with a one-track mind is coldly calculating when he inhales the fragrance of apple blossoms. The pink and white explosions of bloom on an overgrown farm site in May will mature in October windfalls. If there is a stream trickling down, tangles of grapevines, a ghostly procession of birches, and the anemic gleam of poplar, one cannot be mistaken. Laurel and hawthorn, highbush cranberries, blueberries, and wild cherry all relate to grouse. Flowers tell all: in springtime it is profitable to cruise the fringe woodlands.

During that wonderful time of year, shortly after sunrise spikes the pole timber with shafts of amethyst and gold, partridges will be drumming. Their muffled thunder seems to arise from the very bowels of the earth: It is ventriloquial and strangely elfin. A drumming partridge is the epitome of springtime, its sound as wild as the aboriginal wilderness, a thing we must never lose.

Now birds frequent dry, semi-open uplands. They have had enough of cold and wet, so the swamps—strident with frogs and grackles—are forsaken. Cocks strut in greening forest aisles. The tender shoots of springtime offer a more diverse diet than the buds and desiccated seeds of winter. Dry brushy uplands and forsaken clearings close to high canopy are the domain of mating grouse. This will be home territory while broods are reared in the shelter of understory and in the warm shadow and shine of late spring sunlight. It is a fairyland where lady-slippers lift pink chalices in leaf mold, and a carpet of pine needles meets the green grass of undecided clearings.

There tiny yellow and brown chicks will forage under a hen's glittering eye. They'll spend approximately ten days gorging on ants and other insects, on the first soft-fleshed fruits of the burgeoning spring-time—and then these pullets of the near wilderness will concentrate on vegetation. The size of quail, they'll buzz over the huckleberries and roost in low brush.

Midsummer finds maturing broods foraging in the thick tangles of bottomland and lush upland pastures. Usually, at this season, dry weather will have sucked a great deal of moisture from the earth and, since there is life-giving sustenance close to hidden streams and ponds, there is a movement toward water. Moreover, at this time, adults are moulting, and this alone requires a retreat into the jungles where escape does not always necessitate flight.

It is a season of abundance: even the predators have so many op-tions that grouse may escape their attention. Any man who is willing to battle mosquitoes and midges, sunburn and perspiration, may find the king of the uplands foraging along the edges of swamps where thick growth enjoys too brief a triumph.

High summer is a time of maximum delight—and pain—for any man who loves the out-of-doors. We have so few years upon this earth to witness the tumultuous seasons, and now another races to its end. Timothy grass is lavender and blue jays begin to shriek. Glaucous green leaves are worm-ravaged and tired in the drugged lull before each afternoon thunderstorm. Early goldenrod lifts its luxurious spikes in the hot noonings, and a legion of insects shrill their prophecy of summer's death.

There may be a wind one day, hardly cool, but still wailing a promise of frost and autumn. The poplars turn pale, flipping their heart-shaped leaves upside down. It is a time to prospect, to train a young dog—to see whether birds are still there.

Invariably they are—feasting on the purple glory of blackberries and cherries: strong coveys of half-grown aerobats, not yet capable of their parents' hipper-dipper flight, but well feathered and instinc-tively wild. The little red ruffs and gray ghosts whir out of cover like veterans, but they have yet to learn the business of placing screening cover behind their fleeting figures. At this stage of the game they'd be easy targets, straightaway flyers. Moreover, late summer finds these chickens of the woodland in relatively open cover where the spider webs tickle and the birch aphids plague a prospecting man.

No matter, those of us who love grouse wipe the sweat out of our eyes and go plunging through the second growth. We know that late

*Early-season gunning is ham-
pered by an excess of screening foliage.*

fall will find birds in different locations, but it is strangely satisfying
to see them and to dream about great days in October and November.

With any other game, the opening day of a hunting season often
marks a record kill; not so with grouse. Almost always, where partridges are concerned, the grand opening is plagued by warm weather
and too much foliage. Birds thunder out of cover well ahead of the
gun and they are screened by the luxuriant growth that has yet to be
cut down by early frosts.

Hunters perspire, try to catch a fleeting glimpse of their rocketing
quarry, and generally fare very badly. In the eastern United States
woodcock may take up the slack, for timberdoodles are found in
covers frequented by grouse. In their way these are great game birds,
but hardly a challenge compared to the royalty of upland flyers.

An early-fall shooter is roundly handicapped. In addition to the
almost impenetrable screen of foliage, he is hunting a bird that has a

vast option of forage. The whole wide woodland is then one vast cornucopia of food. In addition to late-summer fruits and maturing mast, green shoots and leaves are available. Cultivated orchards vie with old hunchbacked trees in the brush. Late blueberries and huckleberries, cranberries, chokecherries, and even poison ivy are hors d'ouvres for grouse.

At this time of year, more than at any other, the birds are scattered. They enjoy a harvest that will not be repeated until another fall, and they are screened by yet unfallen leaves. The guns of early autumn teach them something of deception and they learn to dodge, even though the shot string may be ill directed. Often those brought to bag are juveniles, prone to straightaway flight through pole timber. Occasional adults are surprised in openings, but most of the old birds are too wary to be caught off guard. They are the source of that rapidly diminishing thunder beyond green birches and aspens.

Early-season shooting, if truth must triumph, ruins the averages of great grouse hunters. It is all very well to prate of a 50 percent kill of birds flushed in the skeletal covers of late November (and this percentage is questionable), but how about multitudinous misses when the green brush of early October screens vague shadows? We tend to remember success, but failure is forgotten with ease.

Weather conditions may well dictate choice of covers during the early fall. If a drought has parched the land, swamp edges are very important. Alder, birch, and aspen runs, where the ground is moist, will be heavily used. A wet fall will see pats scattered, taking full advantage of every fruiting shrub, mast, mushroom, and tender vegetation.

In the eastern United States, early-season grouse often frequent boggy woodcock coverts. Indeed, until you move westward out of woodcock range, roughly beyond a line drawn from Minnesota southward toward mid-Iowa, Missouri, and Arkansas, it is difficult to hunt or to write about pats without mentioning timberdoodles. During optimum seasons, in the East, the two are noncompetitive residents of common coverts.

Matters change as the season advances. Autumn leaves spiral down and, suddenly, we enjoy coverts that are reasonably open. Last year I killed the last five grouse I shot at—and yet my season's average might have been one in four. If so, I have no complaint. As covers open up, one enjoys a much better opportunity to place a shot string

Tap Tapply hikes out of early-fall cover in New Hampshire.

where it will do the most good. There is the possibility of seeing a bird for two or even three seconds after the flush and, if we are not too startled to swing coolly, we should be able to harvest a respectable number of pats. In late fall a gunner is favored and a grouse is handicapped.

Grouse are spooky when coverts are rattled by high winds, and they seldom lie close in a gale. There is no ready solution, nor any explanation other than the obvious fact that partridges are nervous and hair-triggered when the woods are noisy. No matter what strategy is employed, most of the flyers will whirl off at maximum range.

Gentle rain seems to bother them not at all: indeed, they seem to frequent more open woodlands during persistent showers. Sometimes, in a deluge, birds will retire to thick conifers and remain there until skies are clear. I have also found them in ledges during a downpour. Perhaps they go there to seek relatively dry niches, or maybe because oaks and beeches often grow cheek by jowl with rock piles on the ridges.

In a dry season, early-fall grouse will be found in thick swamp cover.

Tap Tapply likes to hunt close to stone walls in the rain. He moves parallel to these ancient barriers and flushes grouse with happy regularity. Again, I think that birds are shielding themselves from the weather. Instinctively, they seek the lee of some natural windbreak.

Quite naturally, pats change their stamping grounds with the advent of cooler weather. As temperatures plummet, birds find less food available; they must specialize. A sportsman will then find them where late-fall goodies are there for the taking. No partridge starves, but each season witnesses different types of forage, dictated by the time. It is a hunter's task to divine what and where and when.

The choice remains enormous, even though variety descends rapidly with the first hard frosts. There will be greater concentrations of birds on well-drained slopes where fox grapes litter the ground, in stands of oak and beech, in old forgotten orchards where windfalls begin to rot in the grass. As fringe woodlands go gray and cold, edible green leaves are much sought after. A wild apple tree that somehow retains part of its foliage is more than ever a hot corner for birds.

In some areas, as previously mentioned, sportsmen seem to think that grouse prosper or decline in direct ratio to the supply of apples. The idea is quite as illogical as old market hunter Fred Bucklin's theory that birds were doomed when the great chestnut trees succumbed to blight. In the beginning of it all we had no apples, and yet partridges prospered. There is little doubt that they could get along without apples today, so this fruit, together with its buds and leaves, is no more than a heaven-sent extra.

Nonetheless, a scattering of ancient apple trees in onetime farm country bodes well for a shooter. Aspen, wild cherry, birch, and such time-honored standby species as wild grapes, barberries, wintergreen, thorn apple, bittersweet, and even poison ivy are important. The list is formidable: in New York, research technicians identified 994 plants, each of which serves as grouse fodder.

Neglected farm sites invariably play host to grouse, but the perimeters of working farms can be quite as attractive. The use of pesticides may be a factor in limiting the grouse population, and the inorganic fertilizers certainly do no great benefit for wild creatures. The edges of a well-run farm where fields are treated with natural manure will produce more pats than any comparable acreage fertilized with inorganic chemicals. This is logical, since organic fertilizers encourage all sorts of natural growth to serve as cover and food for native birds.

Apple trees in forgotten farm-lands are hot spots. Approach them with studied cadence, and then halt—gun at ready.

When cold weather stalks fringe woodlands, pats gravitate to coverts that offer warmth as well as concealment and food. Dry swamps, where sear vegetation affords insulation—together with a grab bag of berries and seeds—will prove enticing. Often, late in any shooting season, thick stands of birch, poplar, alder, or laurel will be alive with pats.

When temperatures plummet, there is a steady gravitation toward edges where conifers blunt the stinging north wind, and to cutover lots where brush piles offer sanctuary. In this tag end of autumn thickets are treasured retreats, especially where such tangles accompany the growth of forage plants. More than ever, a partridge shooter must take sunlight into account, for a warm slope is always preferred to one shaded and therefore arctic.

Cold, snowy wintertime is a critical season for grouse, although they take the elements in stride. Often a shooting period will continue through the first onslaught of winter, and that is a time when a smart gunner will have all the odds in his favor. The cover changes, but all things favor a shooter.

Abandoned farmland is prime territory. Tap Tapply and Brittany emerge triumphant.

Early winter offers good shooting, for birds tend to flock up and lie close.

For one thing, birds tend to congregate as temperatures drop to bone-cracking levels. Then the fiercely individualistic grouse suddenly desires companions of its own kind. For the first time since early autumn, when broods foraged together, adults travel in twos, threes, or more. Certainly overall population has been sharply scythed by predation, weather, disease, and the attrition of fall gunning, yet the existing remnant of a great horde chooses to gather in little companies. After a winter snowfall sifts into fringe woodlands, one may speak of coveys—and expect birds to lie much closer than usual.

The old market hunters were fully aware of this, and their early-December bag often exceeded that of the logical fall harvest. It was, and is, only necessary to reevaluate coverts and to pay greater attention to sections that promise forage and shelter.

This, of course, depends upon the flora of any particular region. In the northern third of grouse range, clumps of juniper and scrub pine, spruce or hemlock, will be favored. Southward, laurel, rhododendron, and bullbrier tangles—together with conifers—will please birds. Scrub oak thickets offer cold-weather shelter and food. Cutover lots, where brush piles generate slow heat in winter sunlight, may disgorge battering pats. If ice-locked swamp edges and sunny rimmings are strangely bereft of birds, look to the evergreens and the thickest of screening blowdowns. Then be prepared for spectacular action.

In cold weather, birds lie close. The incredibly wild partridge of mid-November is a different bird in December: Now he places concealment ahead of precipitate flight. A gunner may literally have to kick his quarry out of laurel or juniper. Then, when wings batter the air, there is a better-than-even chance that several pats will hammer out simultaneously. This is a golden opportunity for any man to score the double that will make a season complete.

Usually, during the final afternoon of a grouse-hunting season, I take pleasure in tracking a fast-flying pat with my shotgun and, instead of pressing the trigger, I grin crookedly and lower the piece.

There is a secret satisfaction in this sort of thing. I am sure that nobody ever bears witness, and it really doesn't matter. In essence, I have ended the season on my own terms. A bird that might have been killed goes free, possibly to sire a whole phalanx of grouse to populate the fringe woodlands of the future.

After that passed shot on the final day, even though sufficient light remains for more hunting, I eject all shells and trudge homeward. The gun will be cleaned, anointed with a rust preventive oil, and stored away. Henceforth I will hunt without malice—until another season rolls around. It is a wonderful way to end a shooting period. Try it, and you will feel a strange exaltation.

This is rank romanticism, and I know it—but every grouse hunter is an incurable romantic, else he would not seek this bird above all others. I am not alone: my upland hunting friends admit to similar pagan rites, each anchored in the desire to preserve seed stock. We love to hunt this great flyer, and yet it would be unbearable to think of an overkill. Having cased our guns before the law so requires, we adjust a slightly tipsy halo and convince ourselves that, if others do as we do, partridges will endure forever.

Dick and Jack Woolner take a breather in the woods. Even wild apples taste good at a time like this.

*I*t is popular to declare that a ruffed grouse thunders out of cover and immediately places several terrain features behind its hurtling body. Many do this, yet there are a variety of flushes—some of them custom made for a tyro with a gun. Indeed, partridges seem to vary the speed and clamor of takeoff to fit circumstances. Sometimes a bird misjudges, and then a fox drags it out of the air or an inept gunner has the time to place his charge of shot in the right location to kill.

Grouse can blast off at high speed, with a great deal of noise, or they can fly as silently as owls. They may hedgehop, taking advantage of every shrub for concealment, or tower into a clear sky. Sometimes the flush is reduced to a ridiculously slow speed when a bird has to batter through thick cover. Then again, pats drill out of trees where they have been roosting or budding, and this is one of the toughest wing shots known to man.

In most cases, since this gladiator of the uplands spends most of its time on the ground, a flush comes from fairly heavy growth, with the bird taking every advantage of screening cover. Usually, also, this flight is a curving trajectory that requires a gunner to swing fast and instinctively to compute proper lead.

To be reasonably successful, a shooter must become familiar with various flight characteristics and be skillful enough to counter each of them with gun and shot string. Only a few experts are able to claim 50 percent mastery, and even these aces admit frequent failure. Anyone who can bag one out of every four birds shot at has a right to brag.

I have racked up nine pats in a row, without a miss, and have pompously crowned myself master of the king. Unfortunately, I must admit that each series of successes has been followed by periods of dismal failure. A ruffed grouse is the greatest of ego-deflators.

First off, we prate about percentages of hits as against misses, yet a partridge hunter probably flushes six birds for each one that offers so much as a desperation shot. It is said that some gunners are selective, taking nothing but easy marks—but more on that later. We all like to forget early-season sport, when heavy foliage screens departing birds and frustration is the norm.

A ruffed grouse in the open is no impossible target. Those caught in low cover in the middle of an overgrown field are easily racked down: Without something they can dodge around, they often bore straightaway and are no more difficult to hit than so many clay pigeons. Similarly, during the first weeks of an early fall season, immature birds will rise with great dash and élan, only to fly straightaway between the trees.

Occasionally, in thick cover, a partridge will flush slowly and batter through the screening brush with all the ponderous ceremony of a ring-necked pheasant. That's where most of us collect the doubles that we prize throughout a lifetime. Towering grouse are relatively easy.

Unfortunately, or perhaps fortunately—depending on your point of view—the easy shot is an exception. Most of the time you will catch a fleeting glimpse of a speeding compact body, or perhaps you will hear only the sound of departing wings. Even where woodlands are reasonably open there will be little time for a studied, calculated shot. You will find it necessary to swing fast and to rely on instinctive lead and follow-through. This, in the event that you have wondered, is the definition of snap shooting.

Actually, snap shooting is a deceptive term: it suggests that a master gunner can whip his shotgun into action with the speed and finesse of a Hollywood Wyatt Earp, forget about lead, and miraculously dump game. Earp, if he was half the man Western historians portray, didn't do this, and neither will you. Nobody does.

A snap shot is simply a speeded-up version of the orthodox wing-shooter's lead, squeeze, and rapid follow-through. It all happens so quickly that an observer suffers an optical illusion: It seems that a marksman shoots without conscious aiming, but he does not.

Successful grouse hunters are fast gun handlers, but they have spent many years developing this skill. There is no legerdemain in the process, only the ability to compute range and lead in one climactic moment, to keep one's head down on the comb, and to follow through, pressing the trigger when some memory cell announces that this is the precise moment.

Accurate wing shooting, unless a man happens to be cursed with a master eye opposite the shoulder to which he mounts his gun, is all vision and reflex. Both eyes should be wide open. Indeed the better practitioners seldom recall seeing barrel or bead: They concentrate on target while every faculty coordinates in the art of bringing shot string and bird violently together in an instant of time and space.

There is no royal road to success in this maneuver. It results as the end product of practice with slower game birds and with half a lifetime in grouse coverts. Skeet will help, and so will trap, but clay pigeons cannot simulate the unnerving excitement created by a live bird whirring out of cover when you least expect action.

Among grouse hunters, the sucker shot is a bird that flushes close and bores straightaway in the open. Almost always this target is rising at a shallow angle, hence you have only to blot it out with the gun—and pull. Curiously, the most experienced of partridge killers may miss this one, because they expect hipper-dipper tactics and react much too fast. For the same reason, murderous grouse hunters of the eastern United States often develop complexes when a flight of woodcock postpones work with pats: They forget that a timberdoodle is slow, and they swing so fast that their shot string is yards ahead of the target—or they mince the bird at twenty feet. A timberdoodle may save himself by pursuing a zigzag course, but more often he owes his life to gunners who are keyed to the rapid flight of a swifter bird.

If you have studied the ballistics of shotguns, you know it is necessary to aim above a rising grouse and below one that is pitching downward. There are multitudes of in-between situations that require subtle compensation, and there are the usual curving targets.

Here you not only face the necessity of proper elevation or depression, but the demands of adequate lead. Deflection shots separate the men from the boys, for it takes an experienced gunner to calculate lead in split seconds and to make due allowances. Losers aim right at the fleeting mark—and miss.

Hardest of all is the bird that pitches out of a tree and goes slanting earthward at full throttle. Our intuition stresses aiming above a grouse, because game birds usually rise. It goes against the grain to

Frank Woolner centers a close-flushing pat in early winter.

INSET   *A grouse hunter uses both eyes in pointing. Success depends upon a fine combination of vision and reflex action.*

shoot under, in order to place a shot string at a proper location, but that is what we must do in order to kill a diving bird.

In some northern and northwestern coverts, this is a very common shot. There, where birds are concentrated in the thick aspens of bottomlands or slightly higher in equally thick conifers, a dog is a necessity. Unfortunately, instead of lying to a point, these pats tend to fly into the nearest tree—and then depart in a shallow, thunderous dive as the guns move up.

There is one additional shot in grouse cover that stymies a great many of us: it is the studied poke at a bird, flushed by someone else at considerable distance, as it slants through the treetops at full bore. In this attitude a partridge appears slim and elongated: it moves with incredible speed, and gunner failure usually boils down to insufficient lead.

Actually, for a man well versed in scatter-gun techniques, and especially for one who has cut his gunning teeth on wild ducks, this should be a heaven-sent opportunity. The bird is usually seen early enough to permit a calculated swing and lead. Unfortunately, we gear ourselves to the expected, and upland hunters look for the quick flush and rapid overtaking shot.

How much lead? Ah, there's the rub! I intend no mathematical calculations here, for unknown factors prevent statistical accuracy. In the first place, grouse are now supposed to travel at speeds ranging between forty and fifty miles an hour, but this velocity must vary depending on whether the bird is hammering through clinging brush, towering, diving, or in free, unimpeded flight. Angles must be considered and no two partridge trajectories are likely to be the same.

Finally, no academic gunman has yet published a table of reaction times that will fit every shooter in the woods. Even if we knew the precise speed of a given bird, and its course—information that could be fed into a computer and matched against the speed of a charge of shot—the solution would be thrown completely out of whack by the human element.

Reaction time, the lapse between that moment in which a shooter's mind dictates pressing a trigger and his muscles execute the message, varies with each individual and is further complicated by excitement. Therefore, a computed lead (granting that we had accurate figures to complete the equation) might succeed with one man, only to confuse another. Each must utilize a personal, built-in timing device to hit flying targets consistently. That's why shotgunning is art, not science.

A few highly efficient marksmen are fully convinced that they never lead a grouse. They do, of course, but the fact is lost because they fire as the gun swings through the arc of a speeding target, overtakes the bird and passes it, before any trigger is pressed. Always, reaction-time lag ensures that the muzzle of a properly swinging smoothbore has swept ahead of the mark. Lead is always there.

Swing and follow-through are essential to success, even in those cases where a crossing shot dictates placing a charge three, four, or five feet ahead of the target. Stop the gun and you will find it virtually impossible to combat human reaction lag. This may be amply demonstrated on any skeet field.

Sometimes we overdo that nonsense about a need to be lightning fast. There is a rather widely held belief that a gunner has to shoot within one-half second after a grouse flushes. Those who promote the fiction are honest, for they admit missing many more than they hit. This is hardly surprising.

Show me the fastest gun in the East—or the West—and I will wager that he cannot locate, track a flushing pat, and squeeze off an aimed shot in one-half of a second. This would be snap shooting at its legendary best: To do it, I'd want an assist from some Red God of the uplands. Give me at least one full second (but more likely one and one-half) to become a hero.

Tap Tapply, a methodical man, once timed himself with a stop watch to see how quickly he could mount, swing, and discharge a shotgun. His best effort was $7/10$ of a second from the port-arms carry —and he was not handicapped by brush, weariness generated by trudging unspeakable miles over rugged sidehills, and the surge of adrenaline brought on by a sudden flush. I doubt that he ever shot a grouse in $7/10$ of a second after lift-off, and I have the highest regard for Tap's ability.

In any normal cover that is reasonably well denuded of foliage, a shooter will have at least one and one-half seconds, and sometimes as much as two or three to deliver an aimed charge at a flying grouse. Clean misses are racked up by those who are startled, overawed by the bird's apparent speed, and who hurry their shots. A second is a sort of eternity in action. Most of us tend to hurry things, and we only succeed in running our heads against other stone walls—such as the splintering of birch trees.

The human eye is a ballistic thing: In spite of its amazing perceptiveness, it tends to center on a single object. That's why any man who swings a gun on grouse in thick cover will see that bird very clearly, yet often place his charge of shot in the trunk of a tree.

There is no sure cure for this failing, other than deliberate skill in looking for an opening. If you are very fast, perhaps you'd better take things much easier. Accept the fact that no man can focus sharply on two objects at the same time, particularly if those objects are at varying distances. Hence the splintered and leaning birch that offers one reason why a bird has gone scaling over the hardwoods.

In more open woodlands, where a single birch, conifer, or lump of granite left by some glacier is employed by a grouse to shield its getaway, the problem is simplified. Sidestep quickly: There is adequate time for this maneuver and for an accurate shot at the departing bird.

Jump shooters get all their surprises in one explosive package which, depending upon the emotional stability of the gunner may, or may not, benefit the bird. Those who employ dogs may derive greater pre-flush thrills, for tension builds rapidly while a dog moves to a point. Some gunners become progressively palsied as they face decision.

At this climactic moment there is a necessity to study the situation and to make certain plans. It is obvious that a bird is about to flush, and gunners hope to divine direction. One should not spend too much time planning tactics, for no partridge is very dependable. They will never "always" do this or that. Solutions must be immediate and rapidly implemented. The objective: To be located in an ideal spot, feet firmly placed, and balance assured when that winged thunderbolt launches.

Two men can cover the exits with greatest ease, one moving in to right or left of the dog after the other has positioned himself above and beyond the tangle of cover that evidently hides a bird. Converging from two sides of a triangle, with the pointer at the apex, is a deadly maneuver. In thick alder, bullbrier, or laurel, one man may follow the dog while the other remains in the clear as flanker, hopefully prepared to bust any target that shows.

Jump shooters may never experience the trembling heebie-jeebies occasioned by walking in on a solid point, but they get just as flustered and uncertain when a bird is seen on the ground before it launches into flight. Almost every time I spot a grouse pattering through the underbrush, I miss when it vaults into the air. Those flyers tumbled in a mist of fine feathers are more than usually appreciated, because they are a minority.

There is no average shot at a grouse, for the very reason that all partridges are individuals. At times, and for no apparent reason, birds will lie close and will practically knock your gun aside as they batter into the air. Again, there are days when every biddy seems to flush wild, slanting over the hardwoods beyond reasonable shooting range.

Highly successful grouse hunters sometimes are accused of taking nothing but sucker shots, and I suppose that a few actually wait for the easy belt at a towering or straightaway bird. I have never met any of these nerveless individuals, and I suspect that their score at the end of a season would be low, albeit equally low in the number of shells expended per bird reduced to possession. All of which leads to an old problem: Which shots should be attempted, and which passed up?

Initially, any grouse hunter who shoots a bird on the ground should be hanged by the unmentionables for an indefinite period. Ground-hogging is the prerogative of an eager youngster who has had no grounding in ethics, or of the pot hunter and poacher. An erring boy may be saved, but the others are beyond any preaching. They are probably too inept to score a clean wing shot anyway.

Wing shooting is an art, but it incorporates no miracles. Therefore, the only bird that should be passed up is one seen at questionable range. In this case a lucky pellet *might* hit the grouse and bring it down, or an unlucky sphere of lead *might* wound the bird and cause its death far beyond the hunter's reach. As sportsmen, I don't think we ought to tinker with might-do-this or might-do-that.

If a partridge is within practical range, even though screened by foliage, a gunner has every right to take a poke at it. Multitudes of birds are downed, annually, by scatter-gun experts who maintain lead and follow-through as their target disappears in a tangle of brush and foliage. Fine bird shot will penetrate surprisingly well, so principal requirements are effective range and the ability to track a target.

I shoot whenever I have a mark within adequate range, even if that mark is but a nebulous shadow in the screening foliage of early fall. I do not shoot when a bird towers at forty yards, which is maximum range for my open-bored shotgun. A kill would be feasible, although surprising, at that distance, yet I feel that a disabling shot would be more likely.

A gunner must decide for himself, but anyone who loves this greatest bird of the American uplands is unlikely to reach any other decision: Shoot whenever the quarry is within range, regardless of cover—but hold fire when a kill must depend upon lucky pellets. I do not believe in that much luck.

For a grouse hunter, the greatest moment in this world is that atom of time in which a trigger is pressed, a shot booms in the immaculate stillness of the woods, and a fleeting bird becomes immobile in a puff of smokelike feathers. Often a shot taken at the last moment as a pat plunges through screening foliage will be guaranteed effective by the thump of the bird as it plunges to earth.

Sometimes a mortally wounded grouse will disclose its location with a spasm of fluttering wingbeats. Some maintain that this is the norm, but it is not. The same adviser usually declares that a downed pat is fairly easy to find. The exact opposite is true.

If you think you're on, yet see no drifting feathers and hear nothing after the shot, search diligently. Those who are favored with good retrievers find lots of grouse they had written off as misses, and jump shooters harvest biddies apparently healthy at last glimpse.

Lacking a dog, you will lose an occasional partridge—say one out of a dozen. This is one of the handicaps associated with jump shooting, and I offer no panacea. The dogless hunter who declares that he never loses a cripple cannot have had much experience in the uplands, or else he is a liar. Personally, I have often wished for an instant dog, one that I could whisk out of a billfold or watch pocket.

If a grouse quite obviously is wounded and prone to run, try to anchor it with a second shot. I do not shoot healthy birds on the ground, but I will blast away at any partridge that has been brought to earth and is scuttling into concealing underbrush. Wounded and unretrieved game scars a man's conscience.

If you are lucky, a winged bird will fall into a solitary juniper bush, an isolated clump of laurel, or a brush pile—where it will hide without further ado. By probing the recesses of this jungle island, you should be able to find the quarry and administer a proper *coup de grâce*. Birds will worm under stone walls, beneath a leaning tree trunk, and even into woodchuck burrows. Natural camouflage helps them and they have a devilish ability to hide and freeze. They display no evidence of pain, but they are very adept at hiding.

On many occasions I have spent hours hunting for a bird I knew to be down in a covert. Some shooters mark the touchdown point by hanging a hat on a twig. Others place their gun at this central point. Since I want my gun with me, in case it is needed, my initial act is to blaze a sapling with a pocketknife, or simply to break a green branch at that point where I saw the bird fall. The search is then made in ever-widening circles. Sometimes, sorrowfully, it proves impossible to locate the quarry. That's when I find no argument to justify dogless hunting.

Even with a dog, things can be difficult. Gunning a central Massachusetts covert with Bill Pollack, chief game biologist of that state's Division of Fisheries and Game, I guffawed when a grouse he had shot at went scaling over a vast stand of scrub pine.

"I hit him," he insisted. "I saw a leg drop."

Bill's dog, a fine pointer, combed the evergreen tangle for fifty yards and reported no dead bird, but Pollack persevered. One hundred yards from point of impact the pointer jacked up solidly. Twenty feet ahead of his quivering nostrils the grouse was lying stone dead.

Beaned birds, those shot in the head, will often zoom or spiral straight up into the sky for an astonishing distance, and then plunge back to earth. Some approach the peak of this vertical ascent with obvious effort, and then slip back downward tail first, still fighting to maintain altitude. A few collapse at the peak and return to earth like dead weights. Mark all of them carefully, for these birds will be found precisely where they touch down.

Gunners have always wondered about this maneuver. Why does the bird initiate vertical flight when it is shot through the head? And why does a dog sometimes find it difficult to locate a grouse that has been shot down in this way? Curiously, many wounded birds seem to exude less scent than they would as normal, healthy specimens, just as a biddy on a clutch of eggs generates little scent. Nature takes care of her own.

At any rate, the beaned bird is doomed—yet it still is capable of flying for a considerable distance. Instead of slanting over the treetops and crashing into some remote hillside where the dogs and hunters will never find it, this grouse towers—ultimately to fall straight down. Some feel that a head shot blinds the bird and that it seeks the source of greatest light. I do not know.

Ordinary crippling shots present more difficult problems. Once I saw my brother, Jack, make a classic double—both birds punched out of the air within split seconds, and each leaving a considerable smoke puff of feathers. In this particular instance we found neither, although we searched diligently and the cover was far from dense. Jack's a conservationist by profession, and he is a good shot. That day he was disconsolate.

Feathering a grouse does not mean that you have him consigned to a deepfreeze unit. Indeed, many birds that have lost considerable amounts of fluff are only grazed and—by partridge standards—may lead a long life. Old scars and bird shot are often found on and under the skin of dead birds.

Every now and then, one that apparently is hard hit will flush again, seeming little affected by the knockdown. Sometimes this sort of thing can become comic opera, and I am thinking of a fine October afternoon when Jack and I had bagged a brace of biddies on a scrub oak plateau. We were walking across an open field to a distant rimming when I saw my brother mount his gun and fire at a bird buzzing straightaway over the stubble. It seemed incredible that a pat would be there, far from cover.

Jack retrieved his grouse and, thoughtfully, wrung its neck. "No more tricks," he muttered grimly. And—answering my unspoken question—"This is the bird I thought I'd killed back in the oaks. He flushed right out of my game vest!"

A wing-tipped pat may tumble or sideslip earthward. In the latter case you may be able to see the bird extending its feet and craning its astute head, looking for a crash-landing site. Get there fast, and forget dignity. Your quarry will be running one blink after touchdown, looking for a hiding place.

A partridge that has been hit may indicate the fact in several ways. Usually one sees a puff of feathers. If the bird shudders, slows down, and hovers, it is hard hit. Similarly, when a grouse drops its legs after a shot, you can be pretty certain that it will be dead shortly after landing. Unfortunately, some mortally wounded birds can scale for appreciable distances, where they will be difficult to find, with or without a dog.

The target that tumbles end over end is more likely to be wounded than one that sails inert after the smoke puff of feathers denotes a direct hit. A broken wing will cause that cartwheeling motion, and a broken wing never kept a determined grouse from running on the ground.

Some hunters, probably fishermen in disguise, engage in a measure of gentle prevarication. Perhaps I am unduly harsh when I say that it is next to impossible for anyone to tell the sex of a grouse in flight. Certainly a sharp-eyed gunner might note extraordinarily long tail feathers, usually the mark of a male, and there is some proof that a cockbird is likely to tower.

Against this is the fact that measurement of tail feathers is just one checkpoint, and is not always completely accurate. Moreover, while a cock may prefer to tower, terrain and escape cover will dictate evasive flight patterns initiated by male or female. Finally, the hurtling bird is seen clearly for so short a time that all impressions are fragmentary. Color is no criterion; size is deceptive.

Beaned (head-shot) grouse may tower, but will always be found right at point of touchdown.

Every bird is admired after it is brought down.

Immature grouse are most difficult to sex, even when they are reduced to possession. Shooters sometimes collect juveniles so small and
poorly developed that they must be the result of late broods. Without
dissection, it is quite impossible to determine sex.

Although a man who is intrigued by the ecology of our great game
bird may want to log every item of data about each kill, I think most
of us are more interested in the immediate care of grouse brought to
bag. A partridge is a prize; hence it should be accorded flawless post-
kill attention.

The sooner a downed bird is field-dressed, the better. Many top
hands clean pats right after they have been killed, or at least on the
same calendar day. To delay this operation ensures that intestinal
juices, punctured by shot, will seep into the flesh and cause a measure
of souring. "Gamey" birds are those that have been neglected.

Some like to hang grouse for a certain period. Hal Lyman, for
example, feels that they should be hung for two days at the very least,
except in very hot weather. He field-dresses a bird when it is killed,
places an apple in the body cavity, and hangs it for the requisite
period before plucking and cooking—or before it is deposited in a
deepfreeze unit.

I agree—up to a point. Any bird should be field-dressed quickly to
avoid the souring process. Do this in the field, or immediately upon
arrival at home. I differ from Hal only in that I consider hanging
unnecessary. My birds are drawn, plucked, and quick-frozen in the
shortest possible time.

Unless they are shredded by shot, do not discard hearts, livers, and
gizzards. All are delicious when fried or braised. They can be incor-
porated into the dressing when grouse are cooked whole, and this is
my usual intention—for our modern, abbreviated bag limits seldom
make it possible to accumulate enough hearts and livers to make a
meal in themselves.

I am not going to burden you with a chapter, or even a long dis-
sertation, on the preparation of grouse for table. You will find a
library chock full of books on the cooking of game, some of them
admirable and others based on a compilation of ancient recipes. All
blueprint ways and means to prepare a bird that, too often, is pro-
faned by inept cookery. The flesh of our grouse, properly harvested
and dressed, is as sweet as any that mankind has sampled.

In fact, I have little patience with those philistines who maintain that "a partridge is tough, all breast, and dry." Gourmet chefs know better. A well-prepared grouse is food fit for the gods: It is tender, white flesh touched with the fragrance of the American wilderness; it is never a revolutionary departure in taste, but only a palate-tingling nuance of flavor. Those who dine on partridges, well prepared, invariably ask for seconds.

The secret lies in a retention of moisture. There are heavenly recipes that dictate the use of wine or herbs and spices, yet no exotic condiment is required as camouflage. I simply stuff a bird with a mixture of boiled potato, crumbled toast, chopped onion, whipped eggs, and diced hearts and gizzards. Stir in at least one-eighth of a pound of melted butter for each grouse, and complete the formula with a dash of Bell's seasoning.

Wrap the stuffed birds in aluminum foil—the greatest aid to a do-it-yourself chef since some ancient Chinese discovered the beneficial effect of fire on flesh—and bake for two hours at 300 degrees. That wet dressing, confined by foil wrapping, will tenderize the bird's flesh as thoroughly as a pressure cooker. Complete the job by removing the foil and browning under a broiler for three or four minutes prior to serving. You'll enjoy every shred of the tender, white meat—including drumsticks, neck, and that which scaled over the birches last.

In any grouse hunter's log, a double is a great event. This, of course, occurs when a brace of birds boils out simultaneously and you anchor both with as many shots. It is a neat trick because it requires skillful gun handling, because modern shooters rarely get an opportunity to attempt the coup, and because cover usually is thick enough to shield at least one of the pair.

A double is *not* scored when two pats jump at intervals and are killed with two shots. Unwritten law states that both must be airborne at once. This very year I berated myself for snapping a grouse that came out one split second ahead of another: If I had waited one blink of an eye, both would have been towering, and I might have had opportunity to boast. As it was, I got two, but they were back-to-back singles.

Again, on the very last day of the shooting season, a brace thundered out of a juniper island. I swung on the closest and dumped him heroically. The other was well within range, drilling through light hardwoods, and I thought I had him dead to rights. My autoloader—protesting twigs and spruce needles that had sifted into the trigger assembly—malfunctioned. Well, maybe I'd have missed.

A double is just about the greatest thing that can happen to any dedicated grouse hunter. Although sporting literature indicates that such triumphs are rather commonplace, they are not. An addict who succeeds is prone to bore his friends with never-ending accounts of the great adventure.

Last year, in the woods, I met a teen-ager who said that he'd just consummated a twin kill, and I congratulated him.

"Heck," he said casually, "I do it all the time."

I spent the remainder of that morning muttering to myself and missing some particularly easy shots. That kid was either the world's greatest natural wing shooter, or the best liar on earth. True doubles on grouse are events of importance.

*J*ump shooters cynically maintain that dogs contribute to the conservation of grouse. Though this statement may be subtitled sour grapes, a multitude of highly efficient gunners eschew canine companions—and the best of these are high scorers. In fact it is probably true that a knowledgeable hunter can raise more birds within effective range of his gun without a dog than with one. Unfortunately, it takes years of experience to become a top hand.

The late Dr. Henry B. Bigelow of Concord, Massachusetts, famed as a marine biologist in the eyes of this world, and equally noted as a grouse hunter among his friends, was credited with declaring: "About the time a man learns to hunt grouse, he dies!"

And: "Guns don't kill grouse. Legs kill 'em."

Both observations are correct.

The deadliest partridge hunter in this world is a middle-aged specialist who has been seeking fantails for two or three decades. If this seasoned gladiator has retained his sight and hearing, and if he is still tough enough to challenge the rough country where partridges are abundant, then he will pocket more birds than the young athletes who could whip him at anything from Indian wrestling to mumblety-peg.

Fortunately, trial and error in a grouse covert can be the most delightful of educational processes. Hit or miss, you develop ever more admiration for this bird. Each season finds a shooter better equipped mentally, if not physically, to knock down a satisfying number of pats.

With time and experience men become fine shots—but it is important to note that they never solve all the problems involved. Nobody ever will, for life is too short. The best partridge hunters in this weary world spend a lot of time talking to themselves after canny woods biddies have made them look like clowns.

Recognizing this, squint-eyed enthusiasts take full advantage of every known fact. There are ground rules—which grouse will sometimes defeat with diabolical ingenuity—but which nonetheless are valid. Among these are basics that constitute order of battle for success.

First, the gun carry. A wild, adult partridge is not going to flush at the word "pull," and he is not going to give a shooter much more than two or three seconds, at best, to get on target. Unlike a quail in a peafield, he will not buzz up into the clear, blue sky; and he will not thrash and cackle for an eon or two, like a pheasant, before going thataway. He's a fast, deceptive target.

Great scatter-gunners may be able to get their artillery unlimbered from a shoulder carry, or from the much publicized cross-armed Indian hold. Either position guarantees a loss of split seconds that are vital and may tempt hurried, poorly aimed shots.

Therefore a grouse gun should be carried at something approaching port arms, ready for instant business. The right hand should be positioned at the grip, with index finger or thumb near the safety catch. The left hand should cradle the fore-end, ready to guide the piece at an instant's notice. Any other carry is too slow, particularly in jump shooting.

Grip the piece in both hands, ready to swing. Do this from the moment that cover is entered, until the hunt is over. The man who can maintain an intent, alert attitude, never relaxing and carrying his gun in one hand, slung over a shoulder or wedged between folded arms, will be ready at the climactic moment. (Do as I say, not as I too often do!)

The port-arms gun carry is effective because it eliminates x number of movements in getting on a swiftly moving target, and also because that projecting barrel can be used to ward off twigs and branches. If the weapon is light, as it should be in the uplands, it can be held in position with the right hand, while the left clears a way through brush and brambles.

There are days when any bird shooter will flunk the course by hewing to a pattern, yet there is no more practical advice in grouse shooting than an admonition to be quick and sure. When a gunner is ready for action, half the battle is won. Next, he must be prepared to

Author demonstrates improper and proper gun carries. The shoulder carry and the cross-armed Indian carry handicap a shooter. Modified port-arms carry is most efficient in grouse cover; others will cause loss of valuable time getting into action.

move before any bird is actually sighted. At this point, be assured that I am not recommending the infamous "sound shot" that chills the bone marrow of a woods-wise veteran.

As often as not, if deciduous trees are stripped of foliage, one will see a bird immediately after it drills out of cover. Even in this case, experienced partridge hunters flick the safety catch and begin their swing with the first sound of wings. It is an error to wait until any speeding pat is visually located.

This is a primary reason why middle-aged, highly experienced gunners will pocket more game than their youthful companions. The old-timer's reflexes are slower, yet he doesn't wait to see feathers before swinging. He's roughly on target at the first clamor of a flush, usually pointing so unerringly that a subtle adjustment places his pattern in the right spot after the bird is seen. Point at the sound, then hold fire until a target is apparent.

Frank Woolner parts brush with left hand, while gun is held at the ready with his right.

Hunters who pause to gossip always break their guns or open the actions.

Hal Lyman essays a perilous passage on a log over a Cape Cod stream.

This can be frustrating during early-season shooting when the foliage is as thick as any tropical rain forest. A bird whirs out and a gun is snapped up, following that characteristic blurred thunder until it diminishes in a final clickety-click of brushed twigs. No shot, for the bird is never seen. Sometimes, as if to add insult, a grouse will tower after it is out of range.

In order to hunt pats with any success, one must learn to walk in the uplands. A great many beginners find themselves off balance every time a partridge goes boiling out of cover. Veterans are quite as likely to have one foot on a hummock and the other in a pothole at flush, but the old hand is cat-quick in recovering. This is an art that can be achieved with practice. Moreover, an experienced cruiser can swing along all day without suffering undue fatigue. I can watch a man traverse fifty yards of thick brush and know whether he is a grouse hunter.

The good ones are fluid in broken woodlands. They are swivel-hipped and loose as ashes. Like wild animals they seem able to choose a path of least resistance through everything from boulders and briers to alder-grown swamp edges. They make the country work for them, always with an eye to the main chance.

This is a faculty difficult to describe, for it is knowledge that borders instinct. A crack partridge-hunter does not pause to deliberate his way through a stand of white birches; he automatically steers a course that will permit him to swing and shoot should a grouse flush. His eyes may be searching nearby cover, but peripheral vision guides his feet so that he makes few serious errors.

Of course it is delightful to be standing, both feet firmly planted on level ground when a pat roars off and away. But this rarely happens. You get occasional dream shots when strategy pays off in the correct approach to a stone wall, a grapevine tangle, or a stunted wild apple tree.

More often, a hunter is in mid-stride when the bird lifts off. Quickly, he must combine two vital actions. He must halt and place both feet on the ground, so that he is reasonably well balanced, and he must begin to swing on target. There will be no time to think about these things: they will become automatic and they will be accomplished— or botched—in shaved seconds.

In spite of acquired skill in walking, every upland shooter takes occasional tumbles. A grouse hunter who never falls is either a languid

Dick Woolner uses gun to ward off brush. His choice is a 20-gauge over-under.

follower of field edges or a magnificent liar. In the brush and on the wild overgrown sidehills any follower of this sport will suffer spectacular headers. Grapevines, roots, and forgotten strands of barbed wire are natural booby traps.

I remember watching Charlie Lyman, a grand grouse hunter and a Harvard don, fall so violently that I thought he must be injured. Charlie was hip-twisting down through a rocky alder run when he hit a strand of barbed wire. He got over that one with a lurch to starboard, but another strand caught him in forward motion.

It seemed to me that Lyman somersaulted. He thudded into a pile of rocks and I had visions of disaster, but he arose, fretfully feeling the barrels of his slim little double to assure that they had not been dented and muttering some litany that turned the air a venomous blue.

Once, years ago, I also cartwheeled off a stone pile and came up with a fractured left wrist. No matter: In those days we had country doctors who understood a burning necessity to hunt grouse. Mine built me a cast that featured, between thumb and forefinger, a customized hollow for the gun of my choice.

This experience aside, serious injury is uncommon among grouse hunters, for they expect to fall and take some intelligent precautions. The port-arms gun carry is one: it keeps the muzzle pointed well away, yet high, so that it will not dig into loose soil. In addition, the gun's butt may be used to cushion a bad fall. Finally, a wise man learns to accept fate and to topple limply when nothing can prevent a header. If one relaxes and rolls, damage usually is held to a minimum. My dignity always suffers more than my body—and I am never particularly dignified in a grouse covert.

Successful jump shooters must employ strategy, so intimate knowledge of coverts becomes a precise art. Any man who is highly skilled works his beat like an old dog fox. Both success and failure have taught him the correct approach to a specific corner where pines and birches meet, to a tangle of pigeon grapes or a dry swamp that is irresistible to birds in cold weather. Where grouse have been, grouse will be: feed and cover make it so.

This formula becomes questionable only where mankind or nature has effected a change. Obviously, a housing development or a new highway (your taxes at work) will liquidate any gunning paradise. A much slower deterioration, and one that hopefully may be checked or reversed, is that which occurs when semi-open woodlands return to mature stands of timber. A fine upland covert is then said to have "gone back."

For all practical purposes, prime habitat requires a considerable span of years to go back. Do not assume, however, that any given hot spot is *sure* to produce a partridge. Tap Tapply brought this home to me one fine afternoon when I was conducting him on a guided tour of a favored covert. We were sweeping a New England hillside, once farmland, now long gone to birch and poplar, juniper, and occasional wild apple trees. Up ahead I knew of a stone-walled corner where barberries hung like clusters of rubies. Playing the part of a good host,

I angled over to Tap and explained the wonders of this particular bonanza, adding, "I always find one here."

Tapply grins like a Cheshire cat, and he did so then. "Never say 'always,'" he suggested, "when you talk about grouse." A sage observation. On that afternoon the barberries were bereft of partridges. Regard such locations as good corners, but never as sure things. There are so many variables, such as weather, time of day, and temperature; another gunner might have passed that way an hour earlier—or perhaps grouse simply are feeding on different goodies.

Tap doesn't know it, but I have read a book called *Partridge Shortenin'*, by the late Gorham L. Cross of Wellesley Hills, Massachusetts. It is one of a limited edition, beautifully done and intended for a select group of upland hunting cronies. In it there is a multi-stanzaed verse written by one H. G. Tapply. I quote two lines:

> When we've busted one in Jackpot
> (There is *always* one in there)

Which seems to prove, as we Indians would say, that my friend speaks with forked tongue.

Quite naturally, if cover is familiar and you have a choice of entry, go in with the sun at your back. This is particularly important in early morning or late afternoon when a flush into the sun will leave you muttering vague curses about the Law of General Cussedness. Impossible shots are frequent enough without inviting them.

Similarly, utilizing intimate knowledge of a covert, always try to approach a feeding or loafing area from an elevation, or from whatever avenue affords the best chance of a clean shot. Two to one the bird will counter this strategy by whirring off to side or rear, behind a dwarfed pine or laurel thicket, but one must figure the odds. Where two men work together, one can plunge straight through thick growth while the other remains outside, ready for the bird that comes lancing out.

Ruffed grouse are not especially early risers. You'll flush some at dawn, but Robert Browning's "Morning's at seven" never applied to good partridge cover after the first killing frosts. Whatever the season, expect to jump birds after the sun lays a warm hand across your shoulder blades, and not before. Upland hunters must measure time by sunlight, not by the clock.

Grouse feed avidly just before sunset. In cold weather they appear

Jack Woolner halts at stone wall to flush possible skulkers.

to dine most heavily during a short period, say twenty minutes to one-half hour before the last rays of sunset stain aspens and birch edges. Since a healthy percentage of birds roost on the ground, they'll be flushed in afterglow, but remember that a minority will now seek lofty roosts and will come boiling out of the treetops in apparently supersonic dives.

It has been said that grouse always fly uphill and that they always flush into the wind. Don't count on either. The bird's course will depend on screening cover more than topography and air currents. Destination may be equally important, for a pat usually seems to know exactly where it is going after lift-off.

One of my favorite shooting grounds is an overgrown sidehill that curves in natural terraces around the edge of a swale swamp. Alone, or with a companion, I always plan to work one contour line from north to south, then to reverse direction on the next terrace, either above or below.

If we start at the bottom of the hill, grouse fly up, because they seek adequate cover. Below, the swale swamp is better suited to pheasants. If entry dictates working an upper level first, then birds plunge down to second and third terraces. Many, of course, fly a generally parallel course, touching down on the same contour line.

All birds prefer to launch into the wind, and there is little doubt that grouse favor solid air if there is a choice. Once airborne, however, evasive action that is dictated by the intruder, together with a choice of escape routes, may call for sharp turns to right or left. I suspect that the demands of escape cover are more important than wind direction or the slant of terrain.

I do not think that a man who is slowgoing in the uplands will take more or less birds than he who moves rapidly. However, there is something to think about in cadence. It has been my observation that any wild creature will tolerate or even be somewhat mesmerized by a sound that is rhythmical. It is the breaking of a regular cadence that alarms game. If I were a pop musician I'd declare that the beat and the break kill pats; both are employed by knowing jump shooters.

In walking up a grouse I move fairly rapidly and—up to a point—without pause. The sound of my progress is quite audible to the bird: He knows that something is approaching, but he is lulled by the very fact that the sound of this "something" is direct, rhythmical, and divorced from the stop-and-go approach of a stalking predator. The bird therefore steps into concealing cover and hopes to remain hidden until the interloper bashes on through.

If, in unfamiliar territory, I barge right on without halting, the bird may freeze and let me disappear into blue distances. On the other hand, if my course is directed at tangles of thick brush or forage cover that may conceal a partridge, the quarry will think it necessary to flush or be trampled. He flushes and gives me a close shot. Sometimes!

Noise, in itself, never seems to bother a partridge. Birds will feed alongside a railroad track where trains are roaring through the still afternoon, or pick gravel at the edge of a highway where trucks and motor cars howl. Hunters, from the earliest days of this nation, have

noted that pats are seldom startled by gunfire or other loud man-made
noises. Their ears seem attuned only to that which is stealthy and
therefore associated with a skulking predator. If a high gale makes
them spooky, this may well be attributed to the fact that they cannot
distinguish nuances of soft, natural sound over the keening of the wind.

In spite of "never say always," a gunner who knows his coverts
will figure that a bird *ought* to be under a specific wild apple tree, a
swirl of grapevines, a laurel thicket, a juniper carpeted corner, or a
clump of barberries. In this case grand strategy should include a hyp-
notically cadenced approach, terminated by a sudden halt at that
point where all indications point to a clean shot if a bird is there
and can be startled into flushing.

This technique is all important whenever a blowdown, a brush pile,
or a fence bars the gunner's path. To amble straight up to a wall or
fence, and then to clamber over it without pausing to test the nerve
of possible skulkers, is the mark of an amateur. As you are straddling
the wall, or perhaps getting speared in various tender parts of the
anatomy by rusty spikes of barbed wire, a bird is sure to go rocketing off, alarmed by the break in cadence.

Halt! Be prepared for a full thirty seconds, and then take one more
step. Halt again! Often that second step will be the final straw that
demolishes a grouse's composure. He'll boil out and you'll be there,
flat-footed, ready to swing a potent gun.

When birds are flushed and missed, or when events conspire to deny
so much as a quick shot, there is a better than even chance that they
can be moved again. It takes a great deal of energy for a short-winged,
heavy-bodied grouse to lift off and whir away on an average hundred-
yard flight. On the second flush the bird will lie closer, and it may be
even more obliging the third time around—unless, by that time, the
gunner's approach has been so thoroughly bungled that the frightened pat is in a state of nervous jitters.

In a follow-up, error lies in the realm of caution. If you proceed in
fits and starts, the bird—although weary—is likely to flush well out of
range. Whenever the markdown is reasonably accurate, proceed at a
normal rate of speed and do so with particular attention to a studied
cadence. Never vary this rhythm, and plan the exact spot to stop.

Perhaps, by this time, you will have tramped beyond the hiding
bird. Maybe that biddy scaled farther into cover, and almost certainly
he has run to right or left. But, if a shooter is anywhere near him when

that sound cadence is interrupted, immediate action will follow. Needless to say, it is a source of vast satisfaction to outwit a partridge and to find oneself positioned in the right place, at the right time.

Some hunters, and they never enjoy the utmost in sport, patrol back roads in motor vehicles. Certainly pats come to such roads to collect gravel, or simply to forage in border brush. I think it hardly heroic to motor down a country lane until a bird is spotted, and then to bail out with guns blazing. Many do just this: they collect juveniles, and a few erring adults—and then they are proud of their accomplishments. In a gentler age, this practice was called "riding a fender." Since the fenders of modern motor vehicles usually are faired into streamlined bodies, I'll be crude and call road hunting lousy sportsmanship.

Wilderness tote roads are another thing, especially where the gunner's transportation is his own two legs. These trails, after years of neglect, are no more than openings in the woods—edges, if you will. Usually they lead to old slashings, woodlots, or cranberry bogs.

Grouse like to feed and loaf in the vicinity of such forgotten roads and game trails, and a man can get some fast shooting by following the ancient traces. Slashings and woodlots are quite as productive, although a partridge in a slashing is apt to be rather wild: birds instinctively guard against good visibility in a relatively open area.

Happily unpredictable, the grouse of woodlot or slashing *may* lie very tight if he decides to hole up in a brush pile or blowdown. It is always profitable to inspect such locations, even to give a brush pile a kick after the manner of a boy jumping cottontail rabbits.

When light snow falls during an open shooting season on ruffed grouse, a dogless hunter who knows his business can harvest birds at a fabulous rate. Tracks indicate the presence of a partridge, and one can look ahead to gauge cover and decide the probable location of a hiding biddy. Snowbound grouse lie tighter than those on open ground, so the winter shooter often flushes his game close at hand. Moreover, pats become more sociable when temperatures plummet, hence snowtime often finds several birds foraging together.

In jump shooting, two guns are more effective than one, but I think that more than two tend to get in one another's way. If a pair of hunters find it possible to work together, they'll harvest more birds for the time spent afield than would the same two individuals pursuing separate courses in the same covert.

Author snaps shot at an early-winter pat that blasted out of a blowdown.

The trick lies in teamwork and confidence. Those who work well together generally gear themselves to a common speed. It is seldom profitable, and often irritating, for a fast-moving shooter to team with a deliberate, slow-moving partner. Each may be highly skilled and equally efficient, but the difference in pace cancels out their effectiveness as a team.

A grouse hunter must know that his colleague is conscious of gun safety, and he must always be aware of his partner's position. Fluorescent orange caps or gaudy shirts help to pinpoint shooters, and a recognition whistle, such as a rendition of the quail's piercing "bobwhite," may be used. Personally, I dislike shouting in the uplands, but if I lose my companion and a whistle seems lost in the shuffling wilderness, then I will set things to rights with one yelp of his given name. When he answers, with whistle or shout, I sign off by chirping

"Okay!" We have established location, and common sense will dictate the shots that can be attempted.

For example, I rarely blink an eye when my brother, Jack, crumples a grouse that has towered well over my head. I know that he is aware of my position and that the shot string is up and away. Often we cross-fire on a bird that has been approached from two sides of a triangle, and then we spend a few minutes admiring the handsome prize and arguing about who was really on.

There are subtleties in shooting as a team. Communication is highly important, but this may be assured by means of caps, hand signals, or whistling. Normally, in working a well-known covert, direction is no problem. In a strange covert, veterans use the angle of the sun to maintain a predecided course or to direct a partner. Many make a point of realigning at stone walls or fences. The first to reach the obstacle halts—as he would anyway to test the nerve of possible skulkers—and waits for his partner to move up abreast. Then, word-lessly, the two move forward.

Knowing where your partner is located can prevent unfortunate accidents, but it can also create unsettling experiences. It is particularly unnerving to see a grouse bearing down on you, yet be unable to shoot because a buddy is in line of fire. Often, after this ordeal, it is psychologically difficult to turn and take the bird going away. Naturally, one *should* turn before the grouse actually gets there and so be ready for the inevitable straightaway. It takes an ice-cold gunner to do this well. Some manage. I often do not.

Last year, while hunting with Hal Lyman, I bounced a grouse out of a juniper clump. The bird bored straight at Hal, whose orange cap I could see winking through a lattice-work of birches. That pat almost scalped him and, fully realizing that it came directly from me, he waited for the going-away shot and missed with both barrels. That's not hard to do. The best shooters in this world, and Hal happens to be a good one, get all bediddled when a partridge appears to be kamikaze bent.

Traditionally, when two or more shooters work together, the man who flushes a biddy and misses—or who has no opportunity to shoot—warns his companions by bellowing "Mark!" or "Bird!" It's a good scheme, although I usually get so wrapped up in the business of pointing and snapping off a shot that I forget until it's really too late to help

Dick and Jack Woolner swing on a towering grouse.

my companion. Shout or no shout, it is wise to get set and to scan the cover immediately after a shot sounds close at hand. If a bird appears, it will be driving along at high velocity and there won't be much time to swing and fire.

Teamwork really pays off where both gunners know their beat and can converge on hot spots. While a smart grouse finds it relatively easy to place a tree between itself and one shooter, its problems are doubled when the enemy mounts an enveloping operation. Usually at least one of the guns will be in a position to score.

On a parallel sweep, shooters are best positioned about fifty to seventy-five feet apart, depending on terrain—close enough to be in visual contact and to flush any partridge that lies tight between them. Distances between gunners will expand and contract, in order for them to investigate tangles that are likely to hold birds.

The better teams require little discussion en route. Indeed, if there are favored positions, the trend is to take turns in the hot corner. Some snap shooters delight in plunging into the thickest brush, confident that they can topple a bird in the split second that it is seen in a nightmare of alders or birches. Usually, in this case, the flanker ranges somewhat ahead and to one side, prepared for the pat that whirls out of a thicket and climbs into a dangerous blue sky. Partners enjoy endless arguments about ideal positions when the driver-flanker tactic is employed. Those who cannot agree always take turns.

Similarly, men who know their favorite grouse coverts develop a sixth sense about the direction of a flush out of any specific corner. Then it is profitable for one to work through the tangle—after his partner has moved forward to take post at a spot that both agree is likely to be crossed by the speeding bird.

Not infrequently, two collaborating hunters will swing on the same grouse, and both will feel that they were on. Quite possibly both were, and yet one may have missed. A postmortem, before evening drinks are served, should prove whether the lethal pellets arrived from right, left, or dead astern. Old friends rarely care a tinker's damn, but it is always pleasant to wipe the eye of one's partner.

And then there is the business of "giving" a shot to one's friend. This can be a mightly ticklish trick, for it implies that the partner needs some sort of edge. If, for example, he has been shooting poorly, he will find even more empty air in the sickening knowledge that a buddy is sympathetic and laying off. Partners in the uplands are fiercely equal and highly competitive. Otherwise they wouldn't be partners.

If a dog is employed and there is a point, first blood usually is accorded to the dog's owner. In jump shooting, the location of the flush is important. A bird that flashes out of cover directly ahead of my partner is *his* bird, until such time as he misses—and then I will make every effort to wipe his eye. One that rockets out between us is anybody's chicken, so long as the shot charge is not likely to endanger a human instead of a partridge. The ethics involved are simply stated: Give a man first right to a bird that he has flushed, but never *give* a bird to any man who prides himself on being an upland hunter. He'll hate you if you do, even if he's ninety years old and as blind as a wax bat in hell.

If my old friend Bob Williams, he of the fast gun, ever holds up in order to let me kill a grouse—that's the day I'll case my shootin' iron and call it quits.

I am tempted to say that a great grouse dog is less common than the Holy Grail, but this is patently unfair. I have not seen the Holy Grail in my lifetime, yet I have hunted with and admired a few wonderful grouse dogs. Very few. Indeed it has been my experience that 90 percent of the pointers and setters touted as big poison in a partridge covert are finished performers only in the forgiving eyes of their masters. Those occupying the remaining 10 percent are a welcome surprise because they actually know how to handle this most difficult of game birds.

Dogs, like pet shotguns, cannot be criticized in the presence of their owners. A setter that breaks point long before the guns have moved up, or any hawk-wild mutt that flushes birds in the blue distance is a total loss, yet the owner of such a crocodile will invent excuses for his dog's behavior and will hate the guts of an observer who mentions, however obliquely, its obvious faults.

For several perfectly valid reasons, passable grouse dogs are less than common, and finished performers are downright rare. Of course we have brought this curse down upon our own heads by demanding a canine companion who can do all things, and do them with the speed and finesse of a field-trial champion.

So far, it has proved virtually impossible to produce a strain of pointing dogs that can handle a variety of species with equal skill and aplomb, but gunners generally refuse to admit that grouse require a full measure of specialization. Therefore, only in northern regions, where other game birds (with the exception of the woodcock in eastern America) are virtually unknown, will you find any number of setters and pointers both physically and psychologically fitted to excel in grouse cover.

This, to be sure, is rough generalization. There are magnificent pointers, setters, and Brittany spaniels that have solved the complexities of partridge and pheasant hunting, employing different tactics to anchor each—but these are the nonpareils: They are dogs of such exceptional intelligence and ability that an ordinary man can hope for no more than one in a lifetime. If that.

I remember a gaunt old English setter named Dan, an almost frightening genius who spent some seven years nailing grouse, woodcock, and pheasants for his owner, Mike Abdow, and for those of us who hunted with Mike in central Massachusetts.

Dan realized a necessity for speed when the rank scent of ringneck filled his nostrils, but he slowed to a crawl when the heavenly aroma of grouse came sifting through the brush. That setter was equally good

Pointer, one of the all-time great grouse dogs.

on woodcock, but he wouldn't retrieve the things. I'll never forget the turned head and lifted lip that indicated pure disgust when Dan located a downed timberdoodle and seemed to battle nausea.

Here was an unusual operator, fully capable of working a running pheasant across a big swale swamp, never more than five or ten yards behind the bird and finally sliding up to a classic point when the rooster was pinned just ahead of his questing nose. Dan knew precisely how far he could crowd a cock, and he wasted no time in doing so.

But tactics changed when a partridge was the quarry. Watching him operate, you knew exactly what to expect, for he practically crept forward when a biddy was running, and he stiffened when the grouse was located well ahead. Somewhere in the complex convolutions of Dan's wise old brain was stored away the knowledge that a pat can't be rushed. He treated the bird with respect, and so we enjoyed great gunning.

Dogs exhibiting such astonishing intelligence are rare. The average individual of any pointing breed, exposed to pheasants and grouse alike, will soon find it necessary to crowd a pheasant and to cover a great deal of ground in a short time. He tries similar tactics on grouse, and this proves disastrous; so you get a good performer on pheasants and woodcock—and a mediocre stalker of pats.

To a somewhat lesser extent, this occurs when a pointing dog is expected to work woodcock and partridge equally well. In the eastern half of this continent a grouse hunter always takes his share of 'doodles, a long-beaked migrant that lies close. Grouse, infernally suspicious, nervous, and spooky, present a different challenge. Therefore a great partridge dog rarely exhibits the same genius with woodcock, and the reverse is quite as true. Only an occasional fine performer will anchor both with creditable ease.

Most grouse hunters prefer pointing breeds when they invest in dogs, probably because there is a special thrill involved in a solid point, in trying to decide the exact location of the bird and the probable direction of its flight. No man ever becomes so blasé that he fails to tremble at that climactic moment when the pointer has become a statue, and the woodlands are still, and—somewhere—just ahead, a royal grouse prepares to explode in flight.

Nowadays, and for the past seventy-five years, English setters and pointers have been favored in northern woodlands. My own vote would go to the two, for I have seen no other breeds do as well.

The late Al Palm of Shrewsbury, Massachusetts, with pointer and Irish setter —a brace of fine grouse dogs.

Irish setters have been in and out, although they have a reputation for hardheaded independence, and Brittany spaniels have come on strong during the past couple of decades. The old, slow Gordon, with his black, brown, and white pelt, is seldom seen in this atomic age.

Some modern gunners bank all their chips on Weimaraners and German shorthairs. These, like the Brittany, are stub-tailed, a thing that seems to infuriate a hard core of classicists. At my skeet club one Sunday afternoon late in the gunning season, an elderly member was recounting his first experience with the Brittany after a lifetime devoted to English setters. He'd hunted with a favorite son-in-law and the two had shot over several fine points.

"I suppose they were points," the old boy growled, "but that Brittany looked like a rabbit stalking a head of cabbage. You know," he added plaintively, "those mongrels don't even have tails!"

Tails or no tails, the Brittany is coming on in grouse-hunting circles.

rman shorthair on point in Ohio. PHOTO BY ERWIN A. BAUER

Some regard them as the connecting link between spaniels and setters, supposedly possessing the better attributes of each—with the possible exception of classic beauty. Since beauty is in the eye of the beholder, this may be a poor point to make. Moreover, one may profitably recall that setters are developments of an early spaniel and were once called "setting spaniels," hence—setter.

Nonetheless, if you check calendar art and much of the existing literature you will be forced to assume that the English setter is America's foremost grouse dog. Perhaps it is, thanks to tradition, but I wouldn't bet much against the possible numerical supremacy of the pointer. Both breeds have performed admirably and both continue to lead all lists of most popular upland dogs.

Setters are said to be better armored against briers and thorny brush because of their long, silky hair, while pointer enthusiasts note that a short coat sheds moisture quickly and doesn't collect every

Brittany spaniels point grouse in Ohio. PHOTO BY ERWIN A. BAUER

burr in the woods. Occasional pointers (and setters) are thin skinned and subject to cuts or scratches every time they go afield. Some pointers lash their tails to bloody horrors. Neither breed is severely handicapped by hard going afield, and there is less argument over pointer versus setter than over the modus operandi of a practical grouse dog. So far as shooters are concerned, this argument breaks down into two parts.

One faction still prefers the big, slow, and methodical craftsman who will work close to the gun and is caution exemplified. A second group demands field-trial class and speed coupled with the radar nose that can pin a bird while the dog is soaring over low-bush huckleberries at full throttle.

Crackerbarrel sessions often degenerate into bitter invective when field-trial fanciers dismiss coarse, slow working dogs as "meat hounds," and back-country partridge hunters sneer at "racehorses" that bounce birds a thousand yards from the gun. There is logic in each charge, yet in the final analysis results boil down to the ability of a specific dog and the hunter's preference.

Certainly a close working setter or pointer covers less territory, but because he is cautious his owner or handler is more likely to get a decent shot at pats pinned or inadvertently flushed. A wide-ranging dog, on the other hand, works twice to three times as much ground. If he happens to be careless, no chance flush will benefit the gun unless that bird is silly enough to double back and present a passing shot.

It is generally believed, in the grouse covers of the North, that great partridge dogs disappeared from this earth when selective breeding produced a preponderance of extremely fast, wide-ranging pointers and setters for the edification of field-trial enthusiasts. I don't buy this, for the simple reason that a crack grouse dog, fast or slow, will come to an immediate halt when the heavy scent of partridge fills his nostrils. Certainly a wide-ranging dog with no grouse sense will bust pats out of range, and a close-working bungler will do the same thing.

Much depends on definitions of fast and slow. A real putterer is as nearly useless as an unguided missile that disappears into the hills two seconds after the car door slams. Grouse hunters require a combination of virtues: speed within reason, so that the dog covers a maximum of territory while remaining in sight and under control; class to provide hyacinths for a man's soul; and the inbred caution that ensures steadying down at the first warm scent of a bird.

Gunners wrangle endlessly about the virtues of a slam-bang point versus the egg-walking approach. I think there is no contest where grouse are concerned, since it is difficult for any dog to close a wary pat at high speed, slam on the brakes, and exhibit the sort of picture point that is expected in a field trial.

Fine grouse dogs may be fast, but they become immeasurably cautious when a bird is in the offing. No fault should be found with swift quartering, so long as caution becomes apparent in any final approach. There is a fine compromise: a rapid operator *must* become an egg-walker after a pat has been located.

Most upland hunters fasten bells on the collars of their dogs. A few continue to believe that noise is a handicap. Personally, I doubt that any partridge is concerned with a sound unlike anything in nature. The bell helps to keep a dog located, and this is very important in thick cover.

Almost any well-bred pointer or setter, unless distemper has ruined his nose, instinctively points a game bird. Given intelligent training and half a chance to excel, most dogs should be reasonably proficient. That few attain the heights of perfection is no surprise. Men are supposedly created equal, yet only one in a multitude is a genius.

Nor is there any way to cull out a litter. Some old trainers maintain that the titman, last to be whelped, is always more intelligent than his littermates. I have seen it so, but I have also seen titmen with no great endowment of nose or brain. Sometimes superb performers develop relatively late in life, overhauling and leaving their precocious siblings in a fine dust of mediocrity.

There are so many variables! A great dog must possess superior intelligence, part of which is education provided by an intelligent owner or trainer. I suppose it follows that a smart dog always serves a smart master.

In addition to this, the nonpareil must be physically a superb specimen, not necessarily large, but endowed with uncommon stamina, keen nose, ears, and eyes. An ultimate grouse dog is likely to be graceful in cover, but some apparent blunderers make up for this failing with astonishing good sense and unerring noses.

If you look back, it will become apparent that most famous performers have been individuals—characters if you will—and perhaps something of rebels. Some of the best are useless unless they are handled by a strong personality, a man who can match the deviltry and the fire of the dog with his own thunder—and make it stick. Such combinations of strong will and teamwork born of respect bode ill for partridges.

Unless a man is willing to part with much coin of the realm for a dog that has brains, a nose, a desire to hunt grouse—and has been thoroughly broken—there is just one way to acquire a good one. You buy a pup after painstakingly studying dam and sire. Heredity is a force to be reckoned with, hence the issue of a champion is more likely to become a new titleholder than is the progeny of a ham-and-egger.

Since we now speak of hunting ability, rather than bench show perfection, it is hardly necessary to insist on blue-ribbon size, type, and anatomy—although class and ability often are welded into one. Look for a puppy out of a hard-hunting bitch by a famous gun dog. Insist on pedigree, but favor a glowing reputation under the guns of November.

Think about color. Market hunters of the nineties theorized that a predominantly dark-colored setter, such as the red Irish and the chunky black, tan, and white Gordon, utilized natural camouflage in order to more closely approach a frightened bird. There is no evidence to bear them out and, since it is most important for a gunner to keep his dog under observation, a preponderance of white is best. Remember that cuddly pups will become steadily darker coated as they mature.

In the field or at home a bitch is more tractable than a dog. This is generalization, often disputed by biddable males. Many believe, though, that the instincts of a female make her a more natural hunter, even though she may lack the stamina of a more robust male. Males tend to be aggressive, a point in their favor—but one hardly appreciated when they attack every other male in sight.

There are any number of arguments in choosing a hunting dog by sex. One is the fact that bitches choose the most inopportune times to enter heat. Of course a female can be spayed very early in the game and this, contrary to popular opinion, will not blunt her desire to hunt. However, if the spayed bitch develops into a truly great bird dog, you will kick your own butt for having arbitrarily destroyed the possibility of a dynasty.

Bay State Mickey, a sixteen-month-old English setter owned by dog-trainer Bob Etsell of Carlysle, Massachusetts. Traditionally, setters are this country's premier grouse dogs.

Having investigated bloodlines and the local reputation of dam and sire, buy the pup you fancy, and coddle him—and pray a little that he will inherit the deep, intelligent eye, the unerring nose, and the genius of his forebears. Natural selection is an onward and upward thing. If you are very lucky you may have the makings of a champion, a gun dog that will make all previous performers look like fumblers. We all feel that way when a new pup comes home, and once in a blue moon it comes true.

There is one way to copper all bets: Purchase an adult pointer, setter, Brittany, or other breed that has been thoroughly broken by a competent professional handler. The field-trial boys take their lumps from countrymen who say they prefer old-fashioned meat dogs—but these specialists really offer the best in the world. A reputable handler will have his own finished performers for sale, dogs that have proved themselves in grouse trials and in the field. Beautifully trained and conditioned animals come high, but cost per pound of inspired dog-flesh should be matched against your own available time, talent, and frustration in breaking a pup of unknown natural ability.

Perhaps this is the place to discuss adult gift dogs. Generally speaking it is a mistake to accept, for free, any supposedly sterling canine. There are exceptions, but a gift dog usually is a real crocodile; something is wrong with him, or his owner would not be so anxious to find a good home for his champion.

My brother once acquired an adult German shorthair named Rommel. The pointer was handsome enough to grace any bench show's ring, and he seemed friendly, although mighty nervous and high strung. The donor said only that his dog had a thing about chewing sheets on a neighbor's clothesline.

It developed that Rommel would indeed attack a sheet or any other item of wash flapping in the breeze. In addition, he ate shoes, rugs, and other supposedly inedible objects, including automobile seat belts and upholstery. The fact that he was a handsome brute hardly excused Rommel's penchant for eating anything and everything. Compared to him, ostriches and goats were pikers. Finally, he regarded hunting with passionate distaste.

Experienced upland gunners who, for one reason or another, find themselves unable to support a prized dog, have been known to place such an animal in the hands of a shooting companion. Similarly, buddies often exchange promising pups. If there is any lesson here, it is simply this: never accept a gift dog unless you are on intimate terms with the owner or—better still—the dog itself. Any other condition ensures frustration.

Having acquired a pup, train him to obey simple commands: to come, to whoa, to sit, to heel—and to consider his master the Almighty. If you have a pointing breed, the dog should not be taught to fetch or retrieve, but to "point dead." A retriever, of course, will collect the game and lay it in your hand. It is fair to note that some owners of pointing dogs want them to fetch game. This is a matter of individual preference.

In training, note that it is a rather good idea to be fair in chastisement and reward. An intelligent dog will soon become puzzled if his trainer is indecisive. There is rarely any need to beat a dog: those who do so may build discipline, but it will be cringing obedience rather than a high-headed desire to please. A folded newspaper or a limber switch is the heaviest club needed, and these should be used sparingly with all but the most hardheaded of individuals. It is surprising to observe the effect of the human voice as a bludgeon or as a caress for work well done.

Nonprofessionals usually err on the side of lenience, but the line between necessary punishment and cruelty is quite apparent to successful handlers. The use of an electronic training collar—one of the greatest dog training aids ever invented—is a case in point. With it, a headstrong character can be dealt swift punishment immediately after it has ignored a vocal order. There is no wondering whether the subject has forgotten the nature of his transgression by the time physical punishment can be meted out with folded newspaper or switch. Best of all, having learned his lesson, the dog never associates that piercing shock with his beloved master! It is simply a painful thing that happens when he disobeys a command.

One should never expect stellar performance during a pup's first autumn season, but a man who wants a grouse dog should work his new pointer, setter, or Brittany on *grouse*. Do not specialize in woodcock, for these lie close and provide little challenge. I do not believe that a potential grouse dog should be trained on ring-necked pheasants, but it is only fair to note that a lot of successful handlers disagree. Pheasants are great game birds: tough, self-reliant, and immeasurably wary even though raised on state game farms—but they run like ostriches, often have to be almost bodily booted out of cover, and are so totally unlike pats that they may ruin the grouse-hunting instincts of a young dog.

A pheasant has to be pushed hard. Quail will stand crowding, up to a point, and so will woodcock. Grouse will not. In the beginning a dog conditioned to pats may be too cautious in approaching a timberdoodle, but most of the good ones soon learn to differentiate. If they do not, then count your blessings when a pointer or setter is cautious.

A fine partridge dog may cover ground rapidly, but he steadies down and becomes very professional at the first whiff of bird. Good ones may go cautious at fifty yards, and old gaffers never fail to tell of tree-points, where the pat was roosting in a gnarled apple tree or conifer.

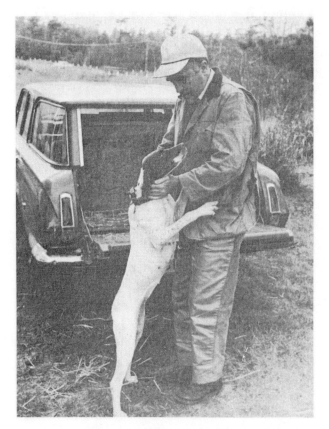

Hal Lyman's pointer bitch is ready to go.

Grouse run, too, but not in the broken-field manner of pheasants. They go skittering along like little old ladies, shopping bent, cocking a glittering eye back and listening to the sound of whatever is on the other side of the cover. Pats hesitate and change their minds; they circle a juniper and think about hiding. Then they go on until there is no alternative—either they hide or they cross a clearing.

Now, if there is one thing in this world that a grouse hates to do, it is to walk across open ground. Granted, he could fly, but, again, a grouse hates to fly until that is absolutely necessary. Now, between the oncoming dog and the terror of wide-open spaces, he is most likely to crouch and wait.

Great pointers and setters seem to know just when and where this will happen. Of course, experienced hunters take stock of the situation and prepare themselves for the inevitable flush. Sometimes, those of us who are not in complete rapport with the dog make memorable mistakes. We forget that scenting conditions may be good, or very poor. Often the dog is operating at a tremendous disadvantage, yet we look for the usual fine performance. That's what happened one day when I hunted with Hal Lyman and his old Scottish pointer, Flash.

It was mid-October and our Yankee countryside had been parched by three months of drought. Birds were plentiful, but the temperature had zoomed to eighty degrees and the brush was near a state of internal combustion.

That was a trial for us, with almost unbearable heat and salty perspiration running into our eyes, but it must have been hell for Flash, who was then in the twilight of an illustrious career—first on the moors of Scotland, and then in American partridge coverts. Water was nonexistent in our woodlands. That day I carried a canteen for the dog's benefit, not ours.

We had approached one of those ancient stone walls that stitch most of New England's back country. Beyond, I saw a slope spotted with junipers, white birch, and aspen. Hal was fifty yards to my right and Flash, quartering nicely, swung across my front. Suddenly two grouse flushed ahead of him and went battering away, well out of range. The dog appeared to chase them.

I climbed over the wall and panted up the slope. By the time I reached the spot where those birds had boiled out I was hot, tired, and irritable. Flash came weaving back toward me and, twenty feet away, halted in a picture point, head turned to the right.

Hal was nowhere in sight or hearing, so I vented my disgust. "That's where they *were*," I growled, "before you chased them right out of the damned country!" And I turned my back, reaching for a bandanna to sop my streaming face.

That's when another brace of grouse, beautifully anchored by the big Scottish pointer, came thundering out of a juniper clump and whirred away in the bright, electric blue sky. By the time I had organized myself they were gone. Flash simply looked at me, and I think it is fortunate that dogs can't talk. Presently he went off to find Hal.

Later that day the big pointer located a bird that pitched downhill after flushing some thirty yards from the point where Lyman was standing. Hal's 16-gauge double punched out one shot before the grouse disappeared in stubborn foliage, but he thought he was on. So did the dog.

Flash was far from puppyhood at that time, and he was weary with the broiling sun and the briers and the crisp underbrush. Probably his feet hurt, but he creaked down the slope and made one cast through a dry alder swamp to pin and hold a nice hen grouse. Without a dog, that one would have fed the foxes.

Any dog is better than none with a bird down and lost. Thus, while classic grouse hunters always favor the long-tailed pointing breeds, there is much to be said for spaniels and retrievers of various kinds. A cocker or an English spaniel that works close to the gun and is sure death on cripples can save many a day in the uplands. The main difficulty here lies in keeping the dog close enough to prevent him from flushing birds out of range. This is a matter of good training and it has been mastered by the better practitioners.

The cocker spaniel is too small for ideal work with grouse. As his name implies, he is more effective on woodcock, yet a cocker may be a very wise choice for the jump shooter who hates to lose wounded birds.

Springers probably challenge setters and pointers as the first true grouse dogs in America. They were the initial choice of Yankee gunners who desired an all-around performer who could work long hours, flush, and then fetch downed birds. Few breeds surpass the English springer spaniel when it comes to finding and anchoring a winged pat.

Of course the Brittany spaniel has become very popular in recent years—with good reason. This is a comparatively big dog that combines the virtues of the pointing types with the unerring nose and retrieving ability of the spaniels. Brittainies, at least most of those I have witnessed in action, seem better paced to woodcock than grouse. That they can handle both (and do a fine job on pheasants as well) has been amply demonstrated.

This very year I hunted with Ed Pease of North Brookfield, Massachusetts. We sought timberdoodles, but his fine Brittany gave me three grouse in addition to a limit of woodcock. Tap Tapply prefers the stub-tails, and I have spent some pleasant days shooting over his liver-and-white dog in the coverts close to New Hampshire's Lake Winnipesaukee.

During recent years American sportsmen have become more than

Tap Tapply waits for Brittany to place a grouse in his hand.

usually enamored of the Labrador retriever, a breed possessed of exceptional intelligence and tremendous stamina, but hardly rated a grouse dog by classicists. Tradition aside, a Lab can work pats surprisingly well if he is kept close to the gun. And because this big brown, black, or yellow hunk of pure brains seems to understand everything that is said to him, he is quite capable of turning in a creditable performance.

In Maine, I was hunting one day with Paul Kukonen, an angling authority who has discovered that gunning is quite as intoxicating a sport. Paul's big Lab, called Hey-You because that seemed a standard form of address when the dog was a puppy, ranged ahead of us. We were working the downside of a southwestern slope, Paul and his dog to my left, about fifty yards distant. I heard Kukonen shoot once, and moments later a grouse came buzzing up the slope toward me. It all happened in seconds: I missed the head-on shot, turned, and dumped the bird as it sliced into a stand of spruces. Soft feathers drifted in the autumn air.

Tap Tapply and Brittany admire a New Hampshire pat.

Hey-You came up the slope like a demented greyhound, made one apparently aimless sweep through the spruces, and went rocketing back to Paul.

"Bring the dog up here!" I shouted. "That bird's down, cold!"

"There's no bird up there," Kukonen yelled. "Not now, anyway."

And there wasn't. Hey-You, in his rapid circuit, had snatched the dead pat and rushed it right back to his master. Evidently the big Lab had watched this bird's flight through a half circle that must have encompassed 150 yards, raced to its touchdown point, and grabbed it before it stopped fluttering.

Labradors are born retrievers, so I suppose we should not be surprised when they do the job well. No breed is more efficient in this department. One day I watched Warren Williams, an exceptionally fine Massachusetts wing shot, drop a grouse in a tangled swale swamp. By the way that pat tumbled, we knew that it was wing tipped and would run.

But Warren's Labrador, Lady, went bounding into the jungle with ears and nose working. We saw her pause for a moment, and then— like a red fox pouncing on a mouse—she leaped sidewise and came down burrowing. The grouse was there and still alive when she placed it in Williams' hand.

These black dogs honor their masters, but they have an intelligence that sometimes is overwhelming. Hunting with outdoor writer Jerry Kissell and his Lab, Cindy, in central Massachusetts—I talked to the dog. Jerry was well up on a ridge and I was coursing the bottomland, following the meanderings of a stream. Cindy was near me, probably because she sensed birds.

"Black dog," I said, "there has to be a pat in this bend of the river. If I walk down there I'll be stuck in the alders, but if you go I'll see the bird from here. Get down there!"

Cindy rolled a knowing eye and slanted straight into the bend. A grouse battered out, became a shadow in the still leafy underbrush, and I blasted a charge of 8's at a nebulous target.

Jerry, away up on the hill, yelled. "Didja get 'im?"

I thought I had, but said I was damned if I knew, considering the foliage. Quietly, I urged the black dog to look. "Right there," I stage-whispered. "Dead bird."

She spattered in through the stream's edge, paused a moment, and came spattering out. She didn't go to Jerry. She came directly to me

Jerry Kissell's Labrador accepts congratulations in a woodcock covert.

and laid the bird in my hand. Obviously, on this occasion, I was The Man, and the Lab knew it. Intelligence!

Golden retrievers, currently less popular than the Labrador, are similarly endowed with nose and brain. Like the Lab, a golden is a big, powerful animal, yet a remarkably tractable one. I have always lumped the two in a single, complimentary package. The big retrievers are great dogs, possibly the best all-around hunters ever developed by breeders.

Although the jump shooter hates to admit as much, there are situations in which a gunner will be almost completely stymied without the aid of a well-broken dog. In tangled bullbriers or heavy laurel growth, in thick scrub oak and even where northern alder runs are so thick as to simulate jungle growth, the single man is at a terrible disadvantage. Give him a working dog and he will enjoy fast shooting. Moreover, he will derive a crowning satisfaction that is denied the jump shooter, a sense of having participated in team action. There is nothing quite like it under the autumn sun.

Great dogs are unusual, and a lucky hunter may own one in a lifetime of fair to middling performers. No matter: every dog is an individual. Each will be mourned in passing as is a member of the family. There is a thing about gun dogs that cannot be explained to people who have not owned them.

If you love to hunt with a dog, you'll never be happy without one. It doesn't matter whether the mutt is good, bad, or indifferent—although you will always entertain high hopes that *this one* will be the greatest. (All he needs is another year of mellowing, a few more birds shot over point or flush, a touch of punishment—and lots of love.)

Regardless of success in the killing of grouse, a man's dog is as much a part of him as his wife and children—even more important in fulfilling a specific need. One's dog is a source of natural companionship, a partner in the nether world of the savage that dwells within each of us, a sharer of secret joy and hilarity and satisfaction in the whispering wilderness.

A lot of grouse hunters really like dogs better than people—especially particular gun dogs with floppy ears and big feet and wise old eyes and a devotion that money can't buy or death extinguish.

Springer spaniel admires grouse it has retrieved.

*R*elax! I am not going to tell you that my favorite gun is ideal for grouse shooting. To an upland hunter, firearms are like fair ladies: One takes a fancy to, say, a petite brunette—or an English double that cannot safely be used with modern high velocity loads. A man can wreck friendships by professing cosmic knowledge of scatter-guns or women.

We are all prejudiced. However, I intend to attack this chapter objectively, employing the arguments of my hunting friends, together with whatever common sense I happen to possess. Ultimately, you must make your own choice, but perhaps, at the very least, I can flatten a few pompous myths. Such as: the perfect grouse gun. There is no such thing.

If this sounds like instant dogmatism, reflect on the fact that all men are created different. There are short men and long men, lean and fat; men slowed by dissipation or sedentary pursuits, and old roosters who are tough as live oak. There are women who hunt, too, and willowy youngsters. In choosing a weapon one must consider physique, psychology—and that curious thing called individual preference.

I, for example, am uncomfortable with a side-by-side double, and so I generally use a lightweight 12-gauge autoloader. Hal Lyman would be lost without his 16-gauge English double. Tap Tapply relies on an ancient and beautiful 20-gauge Winchester Model 21. My brother Jack uses a 12-guage Ithaca Featherlight pump, and my brother Dick swears by a 20-gauge Browning Lightning over-under. We do not agree on personal guns, yet we reach common ground on a majority of basic specifications.

First, a grouse gun should be light and it should fit the user. It should be a weapon capable of throwing sufficient shot in a wide enough pattern to halt a partridge in flight at optimum range. It should be so designed that the gunner feels entirely comfortable when mounting it to his shoulder.

All these requirements may be argued. A muscular farm hand or construction worker, tempered by hard labor, may find an eight-pound weapon light. Nonetheless, any reasoning man will agree that ordnance seems to gain weight during a long day in the uplands. A light gun always swings faster when a man is tiring, and it follows that a man will not tire as quickly when he is toting a meager load.

How light is "light"? The available literature is vague, but a lot of fine upland gunners mutter about any piece weighing more than seven pounds. Taking the 12-gauge shotgun as an example, I insist that anything over six and one-half pounds is too darned heavy. An even six would be preferable, and I'd go lighter if that were deemed both safe and possible. It is, but rarely in a field-grade mass-produced piece.

Bowing to a majority, let's say seven pounds is an absolute maximum. Too few 12-gauge weapons now manufactured can qualify. We are hardly deluged with lightweight big-bore grouse guns. That is why so many upland shooters go to 20 gauge, not because the small-bore enthusiast is a crack shot or an ardent sportsman.

Fit is no great problem. Firearms manufacturers, seldom accused of subpar intelligence, produce field-grade weapons that are tailored to the physiques of average customers. Most of us, whether we like it or not, are average specimens, hence we can purchase, at standard prices, weapons that fit. The norm is a stock featuring 14-inch length of pull, 1⅝-inch drop at comb, and 2½-inch drop at heel.

Generally, in spite of much propaganda about exact fit, the average American can adapt himself to a piece that is hardly ideal by the nit-picking standards of assorted experts who have never had to use a firearm as a tool. Our great shooters have scored with weapons right off the assembly line, and they never felt themselves underprivileged.

For that reason I am not going to dwell on customized guns, crooked stocks, and all the other gimmicks peddled to unfortunates with assorted complexes, most of which are occasioned by too much money and too little common sense. In rare cases one may find a need for custom design, but this is an exception to prove a rule.

Recently a young man came to seek my advice. Literally, he couldn't hit a bull in the bustle at twenty paces. The boy was an athlete, his reflexes were far better than mine, and he was in superb condition. He was, in addition, working his way through college and he had no loose cash to spend on custom guns.

We essayed the usual test. Point your finger at an object. Close one eye. Now open that eye and close the other. Whichever locks simultaneously on pointed finger and target is the master. This lad's big blue eyes were southpaw all the way.

Obviously, he should have been shooting from his left shoulder, but he didn't think he could ever learn to do that—so, in desperation, I suggested the only possible solution. Perhaps he could learn to close his left eye when swinging on a mark?

We tried it, with a big paper target at thirty yards, and he threw that pattern in like a killer. With both eyes open he missed everything but the surrounding landscape!

I am fully aware that this case is unusual, and that a normal man should keep both eyes open when swinging a shotgun. However, it worked, and the youngster is now killing his fair share of upland game. The human being is a remarkably adaptable animal.

How adaptable I came to learn when I discussed this case with Tap Tapply. Tap is also cursed with a left master eye, though he shoots from a right shoulder. He'd mastered his difficulty by squinting the left eye, but never entirely closing it. This, Tap feels, reduces the left eye's dominance and permits the right eye to align barrels with the bird and retain the advantages of depth perception. I can assure you he is a deadly man in an upland cover.

As student grouse hunters, our chief sin is the very human conviction that another gun will correct faults that we are loath to recognize and solve with practice. Blessed be the shooter who discovers a light shotgun that mounts easily and feels like an extension of his arms. Doubly blessed is he who can hew to that weapon and resist further experimenting.

Traditionally, the classic grouse gun is a light, reasonably short-barreled double with a straight stock. Pistol grips irritate crotchety partridge hunters of the old school. I like straight stocks. However, I find that pistol-gripped versions shoot quite as well.

This may be the place to examine that straight grip. It is English, but in spite of my rock-ribbed Yankee upbringing, I must admit its virtues. The straight grip permitted the user of a double-triggered, double-barreled shotgun to shift quickly and easily from the forward trigger to the rear. The fact that a straight grip is clean lined and beautiful is irrelevant. The design was, and is, functional.

Pistol grips serve a purpose too: They are a definite aid to any gunner in a frigidly cold duck blind. Where there may be no necessity to shift one's hand back to a second trigger, the grip aids in holding a gun and preventing cant. I still like the straight grip.

Although many classicists would have you think so, there is no inherent virtue in using a double-barreled shotgun on grouse. I suppose this fetish derives from an English faith in double guns and the Englishman's obstinate reluctance to part with tradition. In any event, it would be rather difficult to prove that a side-by-side is more sporting than, say, a light pump or autoloader. Any conclusion would be based on pure faith rather than empirical proof.

Social status aside, the fine double is a magnificent weapon that boasts a multitude of graces. It is trim, handsome, and, in expensive models designed for upland shooting, exceedingly light. Twin tubes permit a difference in boring, with one barrel wide open and a second modified. Theoretically, this allows a choice of patterns, depending on whether a bird is close or away out in twinkling fall foliage, and it ensures a tighter grouping of pellets for a second shot after the first has been missed and the grouse has put a good deal of yardage between its hurtling body and the gun.

Much has been made of the single-trigger double, but there is a valid argument for two triggers—if only because they permit immediate selection of boring, with no need to push a button or otherwise use one's brain in a climactic moment.

I will not argue with the concept of one improved cylinder and one modified choke as an ideal combination. This is quite logical in many grouse hunting areas of the United States. However, may I suggest that a modified second tube must handicap any snapshooter who strives to make a double at the usual twenty- to twenty-five-yard range in thick cover? Finally, a novice who misses his first poke is likely to spend his second in a quick, white-knuckle snap where tight boring actually lessens any chance of success. Since there is virtue in truth, I must admit that a lot of old stagers—like me—do the same thing.

In some grouse hunting areas boring tighter than improved cylinder is desirable. Pennsylvanians who work ravines where birds are likely to be taken out beyond thirty yards certainly need more choke than

New Englanders who bag their game at an average twenty to twenty-five yards. Adirondack beech ridges and woodlots sometimes call for longer shots, as do the aspen-choked covers of the Rocky Mountains. One must arm for practical shooting.

Unfortunately, fine featherweight side-by-side shotguns have become much too expensive for the average American. Today's best are imported from Great Britain and the cheapest of the good ones will break the back of a thousand-dollar bill. No truly lightweight big-bore double is made in America.

Happily, for the shooter who cannot abide pumps, autos and over-unders, there is a wide selection of double guns that scale somewhere between 6¾ and 7 pounds—hardly featherweight, but still within acceptable weight limits. Most of the economy-priced models ($100 to $350 bracket) are imported from Europe or Japan. Those brought to America by United States firms are chambered for shells considered standard in this country; hence they are functional and often beautifully designed. Winchester's great Model 21 is expensive, now constructed only on order at prices that start at $1,000.

One may find occasional well-preserved Parkers—grand double guns, but no longer manufactured. There are Belgian and Spanish weapons that fill the bill, and many of Germany's shotguns are excellent. Nonetheless, because hand craftsmanship is required in the creation of a quality side-by-side, the type is increasingly expensive. If you have a good one, made before mass production blessed our society, cherish it.

Excessive weight, the plague of many upland shotguns, curses most of the big-bore over-unders, a type that currently challenges the classic side-by-side. A few are quite acceptable, however. Browning offers a Superposed-Superlight that, with 26½-inch barrels, weighs a wonderful six pounds and six ounces in 12 gauge. True to tradition, this fine piece features improved cylinder and modified boring, with a straight stock. The Browning Superlight is a natural pointer, slimmer in line than the usual over-under. It retails for about $450.

Among other fine 12-gauge over-unders that fall beneath the weight maximum for grouse hunting are: the Franchi Falconet Lightweight at 6½ pounds, the Savage Lightweight (manufactured in Italy) at 6½ pounds, and Beretta's BL-1 model, which scales approximately 6¾ pounds.

No over-under is as slim and trim a weapon as the true double, yet it solves the problem of those who find double alignment distracting.

Over-under and grouse from British Columbia. PHOTO BY CHARLES F. WATERMAN

I can shoot one of these creations, but I am always flummoxed by the side-by-side. Finally, the over-under is granted grudging acceptance by the hunting members of the jet set, those who wouldn't be caught dead with a socially degrading automatic or pump.

This isn't likely to deter Americans. Squirrel guns used at Lexington and Concord in 1775 lacked the patrician class of Brown Bess, but they grouped lethally. Sam Colt failed to consult London when he built his Peacemaker, and neither Winchester nor Remington won the West with outworn tradition: they built new and better firearms.

I don't think it sacrilegious to say that American mass-produced weapons are equal or even operationally superior to the handcrafted beauties of Europe. We are an automated society and our field-grade firearms are tools rather than delicately machined and spectacularly engraved masterpieces. Americans manufacture the world's best rapidly artificed autoloading and pump shotguns. For a connoisseur in metal and wood, or for those who love classic side-by-side shotguns, this may be sorrowful, but it is true.

Nor is there anything immoral or improper about an automatic or pump in partridge cover. There *is* something very wrong with the weapon that is too heavy or too close-bored for the requirements of this game. Only a few American repeaters qualify, and this state of affairs must be blamed on consumer demand.

Pheasant and duck hunters abound in this land of ours: They want a ruggedly built modified or full-choked 12 that is capable of firing five shots in succession, unless plugged to three in accordance with laws governing migratory bird shooting. Since most big-bore shotguns are too heavy for partridge cover, the upland enthusiast is forced to buy scaled-down models in 16, 20, and 28 gauges.

A few practical 12-gauge repeaters have been produced, however, and these cancel out the old bird shooter's conviction that a double is the only choice—because a double is the only *light* gun. This may have been true forty years ago, but the argument no longer is valid.

Grouse and woodcock, together with customized autoloader.

Personally, I salaam to Browning's Twentyweight Double Automatic, a handsome 6-pound autoloader in 12 gauge. Browning's Double-Twelvette weighs 6¾ pounds, well within weight limits. As the names suggest, each of these fine pieces holds two rounds, usually enough in the uplands. Among other great autoloaders, count Franchi's Standard and Hunter models. Each weighs 6 pounds 4 ounces. These are grouse guns.

Lightest of the pumps is Ithaca's clean-lined Model-37 Featherlight. This corn sheller weighs a hair over 6½ pounds and is a natural pointer. I have spent many happy hours in the uplands with this piece and I can recommend it as one of the world's fastest handling repeaters. Several other American and European manufacturers offer pump guns in the 7-pound weight bracket.

Then there is the customized gun.

My present choice for upland shooting is a customized version of Winchester's Win-Lite Model-59. This is the glass-barreled, aluminum-receivered three-shot automatic that was introduced in the early sixties and, for reasons undoubtedly logical to Winchester, shortly discontinued. Empty, the basic Model-59 weighs 6½ pounds, give or take an ounce depending upon wood density in stock and fore-end. It is no longer available from the factory, but if you can lay hands on one it will prove to be a sweet upland gun. Customizing is up to you. It's simple and effective.

Initially, I bought a basic Win-Lite that weighed 6½ pounds. That's well within the weight limit for an upland gun, but I thought some ounces might be pared. Master gunsmith Romeo Merlini of Marlboro, Massachusetts, agreed. He'd used this chopper and, with me, felt that its design was far ahead of the time.

First, Romeo machined a short lug bolt to secure the barrel to the magazine tube. We discarded the original fore-end and heavy factory lug bolt as unnecessary. There are no moving parts out front, so this step was practical—even though it boggles the mind of the average gunner.

Winchester provided a straight-grip, low-density wood stock adorned with pleasant checkering, and this was fitted. Of course it would have been quite as feasible to plane the pistol grip off the original, thus eliminating a couple of ounces of dead weight and ensuring a faster handling, racier looking stock. I did this with a second gun.

Merlini then cut a straight, modified barrel back to 23 inches and true cylinder for early shooting, and I kept a bird-caged 25½-inch improved cylinder barrel (together with modified and full choke devices) for late-fall sport and water-fowling.

The Model-59 choke device is slim and unobtrusive. To change boring, you simply unscrew one unit and replace it with another. There is no impression of a muzzle bandage and the entire bird cage weighs less than two ounces.

Assembled, with that straight-grip stock and no fore-end, my shotgun balanced like a dream of fair weapons and was lighter than any of the fine English doubles that cost more than an Onassis cocktail party. With its single alignment, toughness, and—thanks to its inertia rod operating system—lack of any formidable recoil, this chopper kicks less than a 20-gauge double of comparable weight.

True, outright removal of the fore-end left a magazine tube with the barrel attached via a short lug bolt. There is no fat beavertail fore-end, but my fingers curl naturally around magazine tube and barrel. Since the office of an upland gunner's left hand is to cradle and guide the piece, I see no difficulty here.

However, if you gag at the sight of a shotgun with no fore-end, one can be fashioned with ease. I graced a second Model-59 with this sop to convention after various friends suggested that the original looked like half a gun, or made ribald remarks about "a stick with no fore-skin." Clearly, the American sportsman is no revolutionary in the uplands.

So I went to work with a hacksaw, a wood rasp, sandpaper and steel wool. It proved feasible to knock off approximately one-third of the original fore-end and to eliminate more dead wood with the rasp. Sandpaper, steel wool, linseed oil, and a few evenings of inspired labor brought out the grain. Then Bob Andonian, an artistic friend who has a way with metals, fashioned a thin steel end plate, and we had it made. Very pretty, functional—and it'll be prettier when I get around to fine checkering.

Tap Tapply examined this creation and allowed that it was "good looking, for an automatic." High praise from Tap, who is forever wedded to the romanticism of the slim double.

My conversion actually weighs 5 pounds 11 ounces, with the 23-inch cylinder-bored barrel and exposed magazine tube; precisely 6 pounds with the customized fore-end. These are the lightest three-shot

Frank Woolner with grouse, woodcock, and gun that he customized. It's a three-shot autoloader, 12 gauge, that weighs less than six pounds.

12-gauge autos in the world, and weight is mighty important in the uplands. I can hold either piece at port arms with my right hand, and ward off brush with my left. If it were necessary, I could mount the gun and snap off an aimed shot without benefit of a guiding left hand. Try *that* with the average 7½-pound family heirloom!

Fortunately, the American partridge hunter needs no more than three shots, and two usually suffice. Additional loads only add to the weight of the piece. Occasionally a third round is handy when you miss a bird with two, and then a second pat jumps close at hand. My conversion figured in a well-remembered double. One grouse flushed, and I nailed him. Then two boiled out simultaneously. I was lucky enough to crumple both.

Recoil seldom bothers a hunter in the field, but there is a distinct possibility that a healthy belt in the shoulder at each shot may lead to unconscious flinching. One handicap of the very light big-bore side-by-side, over-under, or pump is the fact that it kicks like a pile driver —hence the usual injunction to use light loads. Modern automatics do not kick so viciously because they are fitted with cushioning springs and hydraulic chambers that absorb the punch. Mini-guns that utilize high-based shells to attain the performance of larger bores kick even harder because they are lighter in weight.

Grouse hunters are dreamers: They have always envisioned new weapons that would enable them to harvest more birds. In the beginning, they opened up chokes and even belled muzzles. During the first half of the present century, there was a trend toward shorter barrels to ensure speed of operation in thick brush. This sounds reasonable, yet practitioners discovered certain limits.

There is no appreciable benefit in a sharply abbreviated barrel, and there are certain handicaps. First, if you're clumsy enough to get a standard tube caught in the brush, no riot-gun amputation will help. Second, performance begins to fall off when a tube is cropped to less than twenty-three inches. The difference may be so slight as to approach the academic, but it is a factor. Actually, we tend to wrangle about barrel length when we should be concerned with sighting radius —the distance from the shooter's eye to the muzzle of his gun.

Generally, thirty-six inches is about right in the uplands: shorten this and you begin to experience difficulties. The human eye and hand requires a certain amount of sighting radius to lock in on a moving target, and a tube of sufficient length is much easier to point than an extremely short one.

Creatures of habit and acceptance, we upland gunners have pretty well settled on twenty-six inches as minimum barrel length, with twenty-eight inches a maximum. The formula is correct when it is applied to the side-by-side double or over-under, but it gets out of whack with the long-receivered pump or autoloader. Receiver *and* *barrel* must be regarded as a single entity. Therefore the average auto or pump can take a shorter tube in stride. Depending on receiver length, barrels of twenty-three to twenty-five inches may be entirely adequate.

Variable choke devices that permit a choice of boring can be valuable to the one-gun hunter who seeks everything from woodcock to wild geese. With few exceptions these accessories add a few ounces of weight, together with a visible muzzle bandage. It has been argued that the muzzle bandage aids rapid pointing, and some shooters may find this true. I have never found it to be an advantage.

No variable choke can make a gun all-purpose, for reasons that should be obvious, but they certainly render any single-barreled shotgun more versatile. If I had to work with a solitary weapon for all wing shooting, I would certainly equip it with a Polychoke, or some similar device.

Your grouse gun should be fitted with a hard rubber or steel butt plate, or none—as is the case with many fine English doubles; but never with the sponge-rubber recoil pad favored by trapshooters. These may be fine on the range, but in the field they are a handicap, prone to ruin otherwise possible shots because they often prevent the rapid mounting of the piece. I have heard all the arguments and solutions, including using layers of varnish and thin veneers of fiberglass—but I have also missed birds in the field and muffed opportunities to go straight in international skeet because that effeminate rubber pad snagged my shooting jacket on the way up from port arms.

Obviously, the left-shouldered shooter should not choose a standard autoloader, because that weapon will spit empties right across his face. The double, the over-under, or the pump that ejects spent shells from the bottom of the receiver are far better choices for a southpaw.

So far as gauge is concerned, anything from .410 on up will stop a partridge if the charge is well directed. However, the .410 is a toy in grouse cover. Any serious hunter should question anything lighter than 28 gauge and, if he desires to excel, then 20-, 16-, and 12-gauge tubes are progressively more lethal.

The 12 is most effective, although I suppose there are he-men who could make better use of a 10. That gauge has now departed from the uplands, although it once served deadly market hunters. In our age of sport shooting, nobody needs a 10 on grouse.

In today's America, the 16-gauge shotgun is something of an orphan. Once, and not so very long ago, it enjoyed a flurry of popularity and it is still employed by a legion of middle-aged sharpshooters who recognize its effectiveness. This is a good gauge, undeserving of its plunge into near oblivion. A 16 packs enough shot to tumble any American upland game bird, yet the weapon can be produced in a lighter package than the standard 12.

Second only to the 12 on today's popular market, the 20-gauge shotgun is a magnificent little tool. Its primary virtues are light weight and mild recoil, coupled with sufficient shot to anchor a grouse. Many fine shooters go to the 20—or even the 28—after they have cut their wisdom teeth on big guns and have added inches to their midriffs.

There is one overriding argument in favor of the smaller gauges. While a 12 packs more authority, its excess poundage (in most models) will slow a tired gunner's swing. In grouse cover it is far better to get on target quickly and accurately with a small charge of shot than to blast a cupful of shrapnel behind a triumphantly departing bird. The only valid argument for the small-gauge shotgun is its light weight.

Other things being equal, do not consider the small bores comparable in performance to the larger ones. You will hear that a 20 packs just as much shot as a 12—and this is true, provided that a low-velocity shell is used in the 12 and a high-based hull crammed into the 20. Such reasoning is fine for woolly-minded theorists, but it doesn't survive hard logic. Note, in addition, that 12 gauge is standard in the hinterlands: shells are always available, even in backwoods towns.

It is inescapable that, as you progress down the gauges, a higher degree of skill is demanded of the gunner. An experienced man with a 12-gauge shotgun will kill more grouse than his opposite number, equally skilled, employing a 16 or 20.

Statistically, there is no doubt about this—yet the man or woman who finds a 12 too heavy for comfort (or too punishing because of its recoil) is wise to choose lighter artillery. Handicapped in one sense, he or she will find the featherweight gun easier to swing, with proper loads less likely to belt at both ends, and will therefore place a lesser amount of shot in a payoff location. The precious argument that mini-guns, per se, ensure greater sport is hogwash.

We deal in life and death—however we call it sport. When I press a trigger I hope for a clean kill or a clean miss. Wounded birds haunt me, and grouse that escape capture after they have been brought down in a trailing smoke of feathers figure in nightmares. I want to anchor them—or lose them intact, free to fly again. A bird as regal as the ruffed grouse deserves certainty.

The greatest mistake made by a beginning grouse hunter lies in improper choice of boring. Tyros always want a full-choked "goose

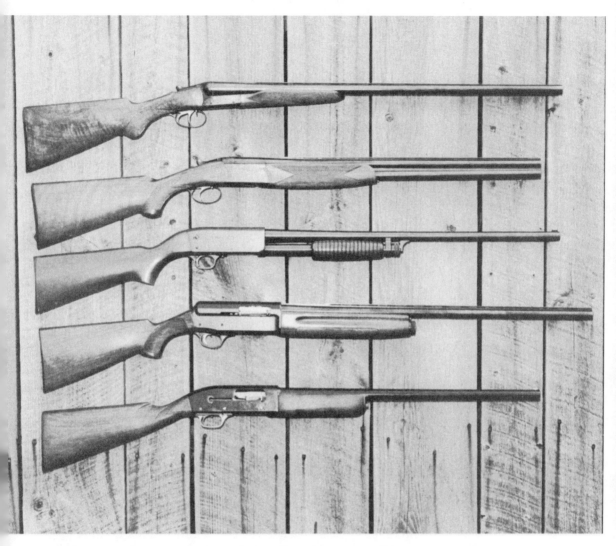

Big-bore grouse guns may be doubles, over-unders, pumps, or autoloaders. Top to bottom: Beretta double and over-under, Ithaca Model 37, Franchi autoloader, and the author's customized Winchester Model 59.

gun" that'll reach away out there. While modified choke is considered a good compromise for all flying game in America, it is too tight for the average poke at pats. Skeet or improved cylinder is more nearly ideal, and I personally see no advantage in the double gun that features one open and one modified tube.

Grouse, in most of our coverts, are taken at ranges of twenty to thirty-five yards, well within the effective range of true, let alone improved, cylinder. William Harnden Foster, whose *New England Grouse Shooting* I consider a timeless classic, preferred one open and one modified barrel. Yet, in his wonderful book, Foster noted that the average partridge is hit at approximately twenty-three yards. At that range wide-open boring is most effective. During the few seconds in which a mature bird offers itself as a fleeting, high-speed target, the close-shooting gun is ill chosen.

Progress in the manufacture of ammunition has added a new dimension. Today's shot-protecting plastic sleeves have ensured a greater measure of control over pattern, and even a tighter degree of choke in themselves. That's why so many of today's trapshooters are going to modified, instead of the time-honored full. Thanks to modern fodder, yesterday's improved cylinder boring performs like the old modified, while modified approaches full. The plastic, shot-protecting sleeve makes true cylinder a deadly boring for early-season grouse and woodcock shooting where, in the past, complete lack of choke ensured erratic patterns. In the future we may see a majority of upland hunters choosing cylinder as most effective for fast, short-range work.

At the very least, making allowances for the preferences of seasoned shooters and the demands of cover, there is no doubt that a beginner who goes into the uplands armed with a modified and/or full-choke shotgun is handicapping himself at a time when he will need all the odds—plus a lucky rabbit's foot—to succeed.

Our grouse is not especially tenacious of life. If you hit one with a few small pellets, it is likely to come spinning down out of control. Therefore small shot is preferable to large, if only because there are more pellets in the package. Today it is fashionable to drive 7½s at these birds. The choice is effective, but I think it maximum. Early in the season, when foliage is thick, a gunner is better advised to use 8s or 9s. The old market hunters, who killed for cash as well as sport, used 10s and 11s.

There are additional reasons for one size of shot over another. In eastern grouse coverts, woodcock are part of the daily bag during early-fall migrations. Eights are therefore chosen as a compromise—small enough for 'doodles, yet adequate for pats at the short ranges necessitated by screening foliage. Gunners who switch to 7½s later in the season do so after woodcock have departed. They feel that somewhat heavier pellets will give them an edge at extreme range, and they are right.

One must also consider the strange fact that shotguns seem to be individuals. Some will handle a specific shot size better than others. Hence, there are tubes that pattern magnificently with, say, 7½s, but throw 6s or 8s in a haphazard manner. Serious wing shooters experiment with different loads and shot sizes, settling on that which—granting that it otherwise fills basic needs—provides an ideal pattern with no holes through which a speeding bird might fly.

In most cases, one ounce of shot is sufficient on grouse, and you can get this in anything from 28 gauge on up. However, the larger the gauge, the thicker a pattern you will be able to throw at a dodging target. While magnum shells in a mini-gun provide the same number of pellets as a low-based hull in a 12 gauge, there are problems—such as excessive recoil.

As of this moment, if not previously, I lose friends—for armies of upland gunners have convinced themselves that there is no real difference between a light 20- and a 12-gauge shotgun when it comes to pattern on target. Those who choose the 20 point out that new, slower burning powders and plastic shot sleeves reduce the possibility of deformed shot and lessen recoil. They cite statistics, but insist upon a cut-off point. Let us, as the late Al Smith said, look at the record.

In skeet shooting we use 1⅛ ounces of shot in 12 gauge, ⅞ ounce in 20 gauge, and ¾ in the 28. These are standard low-based shells, ideally suited to the gauges mentioned.

In order to get the generally required 1 ounce of shot for proper grouse hunting, both the 28 and 20 must be fed high-based loads, whereas the 12 can dream along with its standard, low-pressure fodder. In a light, small-bore shotgun, increasingly heavy loads produce recoil that is uncomfortable to some shooters, and may—in spite of new, slower burning powders and plastics wads—contribute to blown patterns.

A high-based 12-gauge shell contains 1¼ ounces of size 7½ shot, no Olympian height, for it is quite possible to get 1½ in standard, and

1⅞ in the magnum—but 1¼ is more than enough for any partridge in America. A 20 is pretty well crammed with a high-based shell that holds 1⅛ ounces of shot. Even 1 ounce of shot is a healthy charge in this boring. There are approximately 350 size 7½ pellets to the ounce, so comparison amounts to simple arithmetic. The larger the gauge, the thicker a pattern we will be able to throw with the least discomfort.

Pattern is, in itself, a deceptive word. When you shoot at a perpendicular, stationary surface, all the pellets may group in a thirty-inch ring at optimum range, depending upon choke. However, it is well to remember that all pellets do not arrive on target at the same time. A charge of bird shot, as it progresses from a smooth bore's muzzle, resembles a jet of water squirted from a hose: it is an elongated sausage of projectiles, tightly packed at first, and then stringing out at maximum range.

This well-publicized shot string both benefits and handicaps a marksman. If a bird is flying straightaway, leading pellets will find it first, and following shot may then pierce the target, granting that a shooter's aim is true. All this happens very rapidly, but split seconds are important in wing shooting.

Pattern suffers when you must make a deflection shot, trusting the string of pellets to intercept a fast-flying game bird in time and space. Then only a small segment of the hurtling string may actually hit a bird crossing at an angle, while the rest may be ahead or behind. Though skill in placing a charge may ensure that the target is belted with the leading edge of a shot string, and then absorbs more pellets as it flies through the "sausage," it is elementary to assume that the greater number of pellets involved, the greater one's chances of scoring.

Whether you choose high- or low-based shells, today's plastic-tubed product is far superior to the paper hull, which tends to scuff and swell when wet. Resulting deformity may be slight, yet frequent enough to cause malfunctions in pumps and autoloaders. Wet, swollen shells stick in doubles and over-unders too.

Regardless of the firearm and load you favor, any gun warrants respect and proper maintenance. I am not going to mount a soapbox to lecture upon firearms safety procedures, for we are given ample opportunity to absorb the basic commandments. However, a boy who aspires to hunt grouse—or any other game—should be educated by competent adults and ruthlessly chastised if he flaunts the rules. Careless veterans are probably beyond any redemption, and I want no part of them.

Throughout this book I have used "weapon" as a synonym for shotgun. Up to a certain point, I agree with those who prefer "sporting firearm," but there is a sinister threat in any gun. Keep a tight rein on the piece and it is a delightful tool. Relax, grow careless—and you have a weapon capable of savage carnage. Too many have learned this the hard way.

There are certain niceties of gun handling that go beyond the usual demands of safety, and yet pay homage to proper respect. If you examine a neighbor's shotgun, your initial act should be to open the action. No insult is implied, although the gun should have been opened before it was handed to you. Similarly, it is common courtesy to open the action or to remove shells when pausing to trade small talk with companions or strangers in the woods.

Having completed a hunt, prior to casing the weapon and depositing it in your automobile, run a final check to determine that no live shell is in the breech. It almost never is, but one mental block in a lifetime could result in tragedy. As a sportsman progresses he becomes more conscious of the dangers involved in slipshod gun handling, and he begins to appraise his companions.

Certainly there are times when we all hunt with new friends. I like people, but I watch a first-time gunning partner and evaluate his footwork, gun handling, and tendency to place safety ahead of excitement. If a man is careless with a gun, if he lets that muzzle swing across any inch of my carcass, if he slips the safety catch off before a bird flushes—I will be diplomatic, but I will not hunt with him again. My head is worth little on the common market, but I like to keep it in one piece. A shotgun, at close range, is more lethal than a machine gun. I am familiar with both.

Shotgun maintenance, in my lexicon, means no fussy intolerance of normal wear. No fieldpiece ever looks so deadly to me as the weapon that has lost much of its bluing through constant handling in grouse coverts. Walnut stocks and fore-ends develop a deeper, more translucent glow over the years, and occasional scratches are honorable scars. A working gun will show evidence of use, and there is a tremendous difference between honest wear and deterioration caused by abuse.

Today's noncorrosive powders and primers banish a need to swab out barrels after every trip. While most of us run a couple of patches through the tubes, after drying, generally cleaning and oiling the piece, fouling is much less damaging than it was in the past. Rust remains the principal enemy, obvious if you fail to wipe metal dry after a trip in the rain, and insidious if you forget that perspiration contains salt and that your hands can initiate damaging oxidation.

The trigger assembly of a double-barreled or pump shotgun is reasonably well sealed against dirt, but most of the autoloaders should be field stripped regularly, cleaned with gasoline or any light solvent, oiled and reassembled. The working parts of these arms collect all manner of debris, such as spruce needles and assorted twig ends, which cause malfunctions. I speak from bitter experience. Inevitably, such a malfunction will occur when you have a grouse in the clear, or when you're swinging to take the second half of a potential double.

NINE • ANCILLARY EQUIPMENT

*S*artorially, the average grouse hunter wins no prizes: he dresses out of operational necessity rather than for public approval, and his garments are likely to be somewhat tattered after a season in the briers and alders. The first time I hunted with Tap Tapply I thought his attire atrocious, until I evaluated my own. Tap came off with high marks.

The shooter of partridges must wear practical clothing. He needs garments that are light yet reasonably tough. His pants must turn bullbrier and thorn yet be supple enough to permit easy movement. Heavy boots are an abomination, and still his footwear must be able to challenge swamp and upland, ledge and bog. Obviously, each man makes his own compact with necessity, and some compromise may be involved.

Some of this land's greatest wing shots pride themselves on faultless attire. Therefore a casual shooter might think twice before he belittles the fashion-plate sportsman who insists upon a white shirt and tie under his immaculate game vest, and who always wears clean, sharply pressed trousers and polished boots. The implication—that so elaborately groomed a hunter must be a city status-seeker—is erroneous. In addition to a sense of well-being, smart turnout may well impress landowners. The theory holds that an obviously intelligent, well-dressed gentleman *may* be a city slicker—but certainly he is *not* a thug from the nearest metropolis. If this is applied psychology, make the most of it!

It is unfortunately true that transgressions against man and game are always blamed on some ethnic group from the nearest big city. Since country people find it hard to believe that some of their own neighbors engage in poaching and vandalism, a visiting villain must be created. Race prejudice and the villain prototype disappear when a landowner meets any man who is neatly dressed, polite, and articulate.

Upland hunting is strenuous sport, so it is a mistake to wear too much clothing, regardless of temperature. A gunner may shiver, like that famous mule passing brier bushes, for the first half hour of his hunt: thereafter he is likely to be bathed in a thin film of perspiration. A light cotton undergarment and a woolen shirt usually fill topgallant needs. In warm weather, during early fall, substitute cotton flannel, but insist upon long sleeves.

Pants are critical. The stovepipe-hard creations offered by legions of upland hunting outfitters are ridiculous, for a practical grouse hunter has to move quickly and comfortably. There was a time when war-surplus paratroop britches were available at a wonderfully low price. They were light, made of hard-combed cotton, double paneled at the knee, fitted with big patch pockets—and were quite practical, albeit ugly to look at.

Ordinary chinos are tempting, for they're light and quite warm enough for early fall temperatures. Unfortunately chinos are too thin and soft woven to defeat thorny growth. If you wear them, your legs become quite as scratched and bloody as your wrists. Blue jeans are better, but hardly ideal unless an extra panel of stiff material is added to the front of each leg, from the crotch to a point below the knee. Moreover, dungarees are cut tight, seldom feature a sufficiency of pockets, and the material is too stiff for my pleasure.

Some shooters prefer hard-woven woolen pants or whipcords: both wear rapidly and are heavy. They're best late in the season when cold weather necessitates warm clothing, and when a man has become fit enough to tote the extra load.

In any event, pants must be as light in weight as the season's temperatures permit, cut loose for comfort, with enough bagginess at the knee to permit unimpeded motion. They should be double paneled in front, to defeat briers, of a material that will not chafe, and equipped with sufficient pockets—including an old-fashioned watch pocket for a compass. One thing is quite certain: you will never have enough pockets.

L. Page Brown of Lancaster, Pennsylvania, told me about an L. L. Bean pant that is ideal for early bird hunting. We were fishing the

Miramichi River in New Brunswick at the time, and Atlantic salmon were plentiful, yet like partridge hunters everywhere, our talk drifted into the uplands. (Note that "pant" is plural in the Bean catalog, if nowhere else. This is a thing you must adjust to in dealing with Maine's foremost mail-order house.)

At any rate, I bought the bird-shooters' pant and they (it) are magnificent, light enough to permit easy walking in heavy cover, yet tough enough to defeat thorns and briers. This is accomplished through a clever combination of light poplin and almost equally light canvas wherever there may be contact with sharp-toothed brush.

Leather or plastic-faced hunting pants are fine for late-season shooting, but they are a mite heavy and warm for those early fall days when the temperature soars and a man wonders whether he should exchange his shotgun for a fishing rod. I have some Naugahyde-faced britches that are fine in November, but a poor choice in mid-October.

Some grouse hunters favor canvas coats, but I think the regulars prefer shooting vests that feature large patch pockets for shells, together with a game compartment stitched aft. You wear this over a light woolen shirt and it is marvelously light and unobtrusive. A vest or suspender-equipped game bag and shell pockets permits fluid action, yet it totes a sufficient load of ammunition and has space for a few partridges. Some fishing vests are quite practical for early season shooting, but they rarely survive the thorn and briers of a long campaign.

I have one complaint about upland hunting vests now marketed by a number of outfitters. It would be nice to have shell pockets reinforced, because thorny growth tears them to hell and gone within a couple of seasons. My shell pockets are patched with hand-stitched shields of tanned buckskin. Tap Tapply logically prefers an extra layer of canvas, again home applied. If we look like patched ragamuffins, at least we are operationally sound.

In cold weather, a grouse hunter may want to wear a quilted hunting coat. Usually, though, the vest or suspender-equipped game bag is quite adequate and most comfortable. There should be a couple of shell loops to facilitate the immediate location of at least two special shells. In grouse cover I favor light loads and small shot, yet there are occasional chances at a fox or a flock of wild geese sweeping low over upland coverts. One ought to be ready for any main chance.

Game Winner, in Atlanta, Georgia, makes a fine suspender-equipped shell and game bag, available in brown canvas or camouflage. Iowa's 10-X, in Des Moines, offers an ultramodern vest in the new soft blaze-orange Acrilan. The fluorescent color offers insurance against ill-directed shots and the garment is well made.

Boots are a matter of individual preference. Since a grouse hunter walks unspeakable miles in rough cover, footwear must be light, yet tough, and waterproof enough to absorb the murderous punishment of a typical day in the field.

There is a penchant for wearing featherweight Russell Birdshooters and I will not argue. The Bird-Shooter, built on a moccasin vamp, is remarkably comfortable: it has survived the passing decades and will always be popular among upland hunters. Where covers are reasonably dry there may be no better choice.

Some shooters prefer the all-rubber slip-on boots that defeat swamp-lands and upland briers. If you hunt in the rain these may be necessary and are probably most practical when augmented by foul-weather pants. In dry weather they fret my feet, roll my socks into damp, un-comfortable balls, and generally ruin a day in the woods. Perhaps they are right for you: If so, they have much to recommend them.

A few intrepid sportsmen are sure that ordinary woodsmans' brogans or hobnailed boots are best in the woods. The latter scar hardwood floors at home, but they are effective back of beyond.

Ordinary leather-soled boots are terribly slippery, especially on pine needles, and should never be chosen. Those featuring corrugated com-position soles may be best of all, so long as the uppers are light. Too many of today's "hunting boots" are insulated: they may be just what the backwoods doctor ordered for posting a deer in December, but they are hot, heavy clodhoppers in fall grouse cover.

I prefer rubber-bottomed pacs of the type developed by L. L. Bean. These boots please me in uplands and swamp edges. I like the six-inch model, low enough to be comfortable, yet high enough to defeat all but the inevitable plunge into a mudhole I have not anticipated. Some like eight- or twelve-inch styles that provide more shin protection, and this is fine—so long as your calf muscles are not cramped by high leather. One solution is to lace a high boot tight to the instep, secure with a knot, and then lace very lightly above that point.

Rawhide is my choice for bootlaces. The stuff takes punishment and holds a knot better than currently popular nylons and other synthetics. There is one fastening that grips like a determined octopus, yet is easily undone at the end of a hunt. Lefty Kreh of Miami, Florida, a great sport fisherman, showed this to me one morning on Maryland's striped-bass fishing grounds. Later, Tap Tapply allowed as how he'd published the trick years ago. I pass it along for what it's worth.

Lace your boots to the top. Then, instead of knotting the rawhide, pass the bitter end of one lace back through the top eyelet, so that you have a loose loop. Pull this loop up as tight as desired, and then shove the bitter end back through it. Repeat on the other side of the shoe: draw tight, and you have a couple of simple hitches that will resist brier and brush, yet will yield to easy pressure at day's end.

Whatever the boot, and this is a matter of personal preference, be sure that it is built solidly enough to offer protection. Though I favor pacs, one season I went to a lightweight version that was heavenly in easy going, but tortuous when the thin soles failed to ward off sharp rocks. Stone bruises are no joke, and grouse hunting is a rough-country sport.

Feet are mighty important in the uplands. Your boots should be well broken in before the shooting season gets under way. Be sure they fit, and then wear a proper combination of socks. Usually, this means one thick and one thin pair. I like light and heavy wool, but some hikers are better served by silk or cotton stockings under heavy wool socks, the latter serving as shock absorbers. Pamper your feet: they're important.

A bird shooter should wear some sort of a hat—seldom for warmth alone, but to provide protection against briers, twigs, and assorted woodland debris that would otherwise collect in a man's hair or scratch his baldpate. Further, a short to medium eyeshade is essential.

Some gunners prefer a wide-brimmed Stetson, reasoning that the brim will ward off snapping twigs. Western sportsmen find this headgear both comfortable and in tradition, but the "cowboy hat" generally is regarded as an affectation in the East. There, variations of baseball caps predominate, a natural evolution from the snap-brim golf cap favored by shooters of the twenties and thirties.

I like a long-billed swordfisherman's cap, but I do not think it the best of headgear for this sport. We really need something specially designed, something light, shallow-crowned and unlined, with an adequate eyeshading brim. The ideal grouse hunting cap should be made of fluorescent orange Acrilan, a new material that will breathe and so defeat perspiration. Earlaps in upland hunting headgear are excess baggage. The cap should feature no buttons, cords, or other decorations of a nature prone to catch scraping twigs. Any hat that is constantly snatched off your noggin by clutching branches is a failure.

Brilliant color in upper garments is most important. Those who work with partners should be very certain that their caps or shirts are of some easily detected hue. A fluorescent-orange cap flames like neon light in the brush and can keep a neighboring gunner from directing a charge of shot too close for comfort. Activated colors—and orange is best because it can be seen by a color-deficient person as well as by those with normal vision—may soon become mandatory in the woods. The stuff saves lives.

Fluorescent materials were developed during World War II for use as identification panels. Those we used on Third Armored Division tanks, racing from Normandy to the Elbe River in Germany, were bright red. They warned our fighter support aircraft to lay off Allied vehicles.

The same activated neon-red materials were offered to sportsmen in the shape of caps and vests immediately after that war was concluded. A few hunters were interested, while others thought that the glaring color would alarm game. Today's crusade for fluorescent orange as a hunter-safety color was launched at Errol, New Hampshire, in November of 1947.

My brother Jack Woolner and I were there, hunting deer. At twilight, after we had returned to the hard road below Errol Dam and the Androscoggin River, we watched two hunters picking their way down the precipitous slope across the stream. Both were wearing those strange red vests and caps. In the blue shadows of twilight these men were indistinguishable, but their vests and caps were disembodied units, glowing like live coals.

Jack, superintendent of audiovisual aids for the Massachusetts Division of Fisheries and Game, began to research the subject. Later he was to enlist the aid of the United States Army at Fort Devens, Massachusetts, and vision experts of American Optical Company, to conduct a three-month-long survey of colors—both standard and fluorescent—to determine which would make the best warning color. Blaze-orange fluorescent was the unanimous choice of experts assembled. In 1960 Massachusetts made mandatory the wearing of fluorescent-red or -orange clothing by deer hunters—and in six years cut the accidental shooting rate by 67 percent.

Until very recently, caps fabricated of fluorescent-orange materials were uncomfortable, because they were made of a close-woven, plastic-coated fabric. In late 1967, acting on the request of Jack Woolner, the Monsanto Company's textile division in Atlanta, Georgia, produced an Acrilan yarn that can be used to make a soft, porous cloth.

Comfortable fluorescent-orange shooting caps and vests are now available, and they are of inestimable value to the shooter of partridges, especially to those who hunt in pairs in thick cover and require constant visual orientation. An activated orange cap or vest glows like a neon light: it doesn't frighten upland birds, but it certainly pinpoints a friend's location.

Since upland hunting accidents are seldom so grisly as those in the big-game woods, it is unlikely that the use of fluorescent orange will become mandatory for bird shooters in the foreseeable future. Nonetheless, more and more of our nation's gunners are adopting the fiery garments because they are definite aids to a wonderful sport.

Shooting glasses are important. Twice in my gunning career I have impaired my vision by blundering into thorny growth or sharp-pointed conifer needles. The human eye can be twigged by a wide variety of switching menaces, so it behooves an upland gunner to take certain precautions. Anyone who hunts partridges or other brush-loving birds should wear protective lenses.

The best shooting glasses now available are wide-framed, with hardened glass in the yellow tint favored by skeet and trap shooters. Lightweight plastic models are fine, able to absorb much punishment, and can boast the optical excellence of well-ground glass. Pale yellow is the best color because it screens out blue light and thus creates a measure of contrast in shadowy woodlands. Green or gray lenses should not be chosen, for they cut down the amount of light reaching the eye (as does yellow by about 15 percent), while offering no benefit in the way of contrast. Polarized lenses are unnecessary, for there is no excessive glare in the back country.

Shooting glasses are available with prescription lenses, so you can enjoy 20-20 vision together with maximum protection. Clip-on yellow shades may be attached to ordinary spectacles, if you think you need them. Actually, good vision and protection are necessary requirements, with the contrast tint an added benefit under certain conditions.

Inveterate grouse hunters usually betray themselves by livid scratches across hands and wrists during the open shooting season.

Shooting glasses are a necessity in grouse and woodcock coverts.

Sometimes, during the early days of October when the weather is sum-
merlike, I gun in a tee shirt—and then I lacerate each arm to the elbow.
These wounds are honorable, but perhaps unnecessary. A long-sleeved
shirt is logical.

Gloves bother me. When the weather is wintry I wear them until
exercise warms my blood, and then I tuck the things into a handy
pocket and go without. A gun doesn't feel quite natural in my hands
unless those hands are unencumbered—and I assure you that I am
wrong!

We should learn to handle a shotgun while wearing gloves: they protect hands and wrists, while adding warmth to fingers that must move
rapidly in releasing a safety catch when a grouse flushes. Happily, there

are many gloves and wristlets to choose from, and some of these may prove ideal.

Golf gloves are very light and flexible. They are made of fine, thin leather and their only fault is that they are rather short-wristed and therefore allow briers and thorns to gouge perennial scratches.

Fingerless gloves are available in some of the well-stocked sporting goods houses. These are popular in Europe where they are employed by anglers, and they feature adequate material up over the wrists. Of course it is possible to scissor the fingers off any light glove, if you must feel your unburdened pinkies on trigger and safety catch.

My brother Jack solves this problem by wearing a glove on the left hand only: this helps to ward off brush and brambles. The theory is appealing, but Jack's right wrist usually is scratched in November. Let's face it: if you can work with gloves on both hands you'll be a more effective gunner and you'll avoid a lot of bloodletting. Sometime I must learn to use the things.

There are a few small items of equipment that any experienced shooter should carry on his person. These are emergency tools and they usurp little space. For example, while you may know every wild apple tree and laurel clump in a favored covert, would you be able to find your way out in a sudden fog or snowstorm? A pocket compass is a must. Tuck it away and forget it, until such time as it becomes necessary.

In an unfamiliar covert, a government topographic map can unveil secrets of cover while it points the way home. After you have learned to read a topo it is quite possible to squint at the map and guess probable ground conformation and vegetation before you have laid eyes on the place.

Arnold Laine of Templeton, Massachusetts—a onetime commercial rod-and-line striped-bass fisherman, a woodsman, a trapper, and a naturalist—can make uncanny predictions after a few minutes of topo study. He checks contour lines and stream courses, old roads and trails. Then: "There'll be alders here, and probably some old orchards above that farm. I think this is a clearing, because the land rises and flattens out above the swamp." Invariably he is right.

Personally, I want a topo map of any area I plan to hunt for the first time. Together with a pocket compass, this is cheap insurance. So long as I absorb the information provided, I can't get lost—and I can go directly to spots that should be birdy as all get out. A good topo is a diagram of the country it portrays, changed only by human development or maturing woodlands since the day it was surveyed and printed. Each marsh and stream is graphically represented in blue. Contour lines indicate the pitch of a slope, from sheer cliff to gentle rise. Existing human habitations are blocked in, as are major and minor road nets. This is a primary tool of the hunter, whether he seeks big game or that lord of the uplands, the ruffed grouse.

There are two other things that every hunter should carry upon his person. One is a small wad of toilet paper—and I am reminded of a great biologist (and hunter) who astounded a group of sophisticated scientists when he used a few squares of toilet paper to mop up a puddle of toxic material that had been spilled on a polished desk during a high level conference. "A boon to mankind," he commented. "I always carry it."

The other is a small supply of Band-Aids. These can be slipped into a wallet and forgotten, yet they are present and ready when any minor accident occurs. A sliced finger can spoil an entire expedition unless there is something to staunch blood and provide comfort.

Most of us use automobiles for transport to upland hunting covers, and a practical vehicle can penetrate all but the roughest of wilderness areas. The best, of course, are four-wheel-drive models fitted with knob or snow tires, and the worst are low-slung sports cars with only a few inches of road clearance. Unless you intend to park at the edge of a paved road, clearance is of considerable importance. Backwoods tracks are liberally paved with boulders that create expensive noises when they are creased by tender crankcases.

As headquarters in the field, a car should be equipped with certain basic items. These include a well-ventilated box for the dog, if you lack vinyl upholstery and shudder at the thought of muddy footprints. A well-stocked first-aid kit is good sense; though gunners are unlikely to require serious repairs, dogs often blunder into broken beer bottles and have to be patched up.

The kit should contain not only aspirin for humans who find guns too timpanic after a night with bad ice but also needlenosed pliers or a surgeon's hemostat to operate on dogs who can't resist porcupines. Usually a smart feather-finder will steer clear after that first, unhappy experience with a porky. Others never learn: they keep coming back for the same punishment, or for revenge, and owners find it necessary to keep pliers within easy reach. Each barbed quill must be pulled out of a dog's face, mouth, and tongue—painfully, one by one.

Where porcupines are plentiful, use them for training purposes. A few rough lessons with a check cord, an electronic training collar, and proper language should convince any young dog that these bristly critters are to be avoided. One might use the same technique where skunks are concerned, but the high aroma of a wood pussy is never so serious a threat as the barbed quills of a porky. When a skunk employs chemical warfare, it only hurts for a little while.

Usually a dog can find enough ground water to satisfy his needs, but there are seasons of drought and broiling sunshine when it may be necessary to carry a canteen to keep a pointer or setter from dehydrating. Water, in dry times, is more important than food. Like the Bedouins, you will hoist a glass to the sky and exclaim, "Gold!"

The contents of my station wagon always indicate a specific season. In spring and summer tackle boxes are evident and favored flies often decorate sun visors. With early October, fishing tackle is swept away and shotgun shells take up residence—there to remain until first bluebirds return to our cold, northern acres.

In reasonably decent weather, where short afternoon hunts may encompass no more than a few hours, extra clothing may prove excess baggage. Nonetheless, I like to tote a change of boots, socks, underwear, pants, shirts, and also foul-weather gear. The lot usurps little space, yet it is there in a time of need.

Any day in the uplands generates healthy perspiration. At the very least, sundown finds our socks wet with sweat and a change is welcome. Why suffer during a long drive homeward after a fatiguing day in the woods?

The late Gorham Cross was a past master in the art of equipping his hunting car for every contingency. One of his innovations was a net slung just under the station wagon's roof, used to carry the day's bag of grouse. There are two good reasons for this, or some similar arrangement. First, birds should never be carried in a tight pile—granting that hunters are fortunate enough to shoot a "pile" of pats. Close contact generates heat and causes galloping deterioration. Game should be stowed in a manner that provides air circulation during any journey from upland cover to deep freeze. Second, the shooter who leaves dead birds within the reach of dogs in a car provides a powerful temptation.

Some very well-trained pups have been known to forget their manners and dine on forbidden flesh. The habit, once acquired, can become a serious problem.

Alcoholic beverages are to be avoided during any day in the uplands. I like good Scotch and cold beer, but these are after-sport drinks. Indeed, one cannot effectively swing a shotgun (or cast a fly) under the influence of liquor. Those who think that they can do so admit the necessity for a drug, and rarely excel. They are, at best, people who need a crutch. At worst, they are dangerous companions.

Grouse hunting is strenuous, hence it builds healthy appetites. In the uplands, shooters rarely fail to sample frostbitten apples under the dwarfed trees that served a prior generation. Sometimes the fruit is ambrosia, and again it is tart with regression to the wilderness and bored with worms. Beechnuts and wintergreen berries must be sampled, for to pass them up would entail a violation of unwritten law! Upland gunners consider themselves in complete rapport with the wilderness.

But pack a substantial lunch in the car. Of course you won't need it, but you will find that available victuals not only satisfy hunger but provide a refreshing pause just when muscles begin to tire and prospects accordingly are dim.

Cold cuts and fresh bread, cheese and sliced tomatoes, are great revivers. Add Bermuda onions and a touch of mustard for spice. A thermos bottle full of hot vegetable soup can be a lifesaver. Coffee is wonderful, but scalding tea may be more inspiring. Some find cold milk greater than any tonic at the end of a long, warm journey. Personally, I dote on unsweetened tea, Syrian bread, well buttered and packed with cheese, salami, onions, and tomatoes. Years ago, when I was young, Mike Abdow—an American of Lebanese descent—fed me this Arabian-American-Italian combination, and I was hooked. Suit yourself, but carry a lunch.

Some say that you shouldn't smoke while hunting. I do, and suffer no hardship—although it is always necessary to keep a pipe in the left side of my face. Once, in a duck blind, I ignored this rule: simultaneously I missed a mallard and bit the stem off a favorite briar. Luckily, the stem was brittle enough to shatter at some pressure point below the stress maximum of my teeth!

Those who do not smoke usually are nibblers. Chocolate bars are easy to carry. Dried raisins are great sources of energy, and some swear by Spanish peanuts. Of course a grouse is sure to go battering out just when you reach into a pocket to collect any of these goodies. That is the Law of General Cussedness.

No dog should be forgotten during the noontide pause. Some say that setters and pointers should be kept hungry, like yon Cassius, but this is ridiculous. Carry a packet of hamburger for your canine companion or, at the very least, reserve a sandwich for his attention. He has worked diligently and he deserves some reward at noon. Unless you stuff him unmercifully he will work better during the remaining hours of daylight.

The rest is a matter of common sense. Naturally you will tote an extra bell, in case the dog loses the one on his collar. A flashlight can improve tempers and simplify storage on those occasions when a hunt is concluded after sunset.

Now case the guns, replace hunting boots with dry socks and moccasins. Fasten the seat belts and fire up. Home is where the heart is —after the magic of a great day in a grouse covert!

I am not going to the wailing wall with any plea for immediate conservation or management of our partridge.

Granted, he may need both in the years ahead, but history has proved that the ruffed grouse is a remarkably tough and resilient native. He has prospered where other birds have failed. He takes weather, disease, predators, and gunning pressure in stride. Only the destruction of favorable habitat pierces his main line of resistance, and it will be many years before the anxious bulldozers masticate all of America's back country.

Fortunately, the grouse enjoys a far better survival position than most of our game birds. Industrial pollution and landfill threaten waterfowl. Urban sprawl places pheasants off limits to gunners, for that raucous cock of the flatlands covets territory that is equally desirable to the developer. Quail are frequenters of gentle, rolling, casually worked farmlands—again the target of every predatory human from the realtor to the industrialist.

Though land use is harmful to other game birds, our grouse will continue to beat his drums in springtime and confound gunners in November. He will do this because his stamping ground is now, and always has been, the rough, rugged country that is last delivered up to plow and bulldozer. When developers take a hill and chew it down, destroy its trees, blast its immortal rocks, bury its crystal streams in plastic pipes and erect a plywood and cement-block suburb, grouse simply move back to the next hill.

Unlike pampered exotics, this native of the New World seeks no handout from those who have usurped his domain. There is no truce with humanity, and certainly no groveling for a crust of bread at a feeding station. The back country, even today, is extensive and there is much territory for a strategic retreat. If partridges engaged in any thought process, they might believe that this wave of humanity will recede, like that which flooded and ebbed in the Northeastern states of two hundred years ago, leaving them the overgrown farmsites that subsequently were reclaimed by aspen and birch.

Of course there is little likelihood of any land recession in today's America. Although farming is no longer profitable in some of the rocky, precipitous lands where grouse are most plentiful, the fruitful wilderness must slowly give way to lumbering practices that denude the hills, to urban sprawl, and to the industrial complexes that bolster the economy of a great nation.

Paradoxically, a dearth of all lumbering would be disastrous. Even the clean cutting that leaves a tortured and eroded landscape is beneficial if the natural brush is then allowed to spring up. Time is involved, but cutting and subsequent new growth will create grouse cover after a certain passage of years. The American partridge is a fringe bird: as forests mature it moves back to the brushy, sunny edges. Pole timber is a more deadly threat than any combination of red foxes, goshawks, horned owls, and wet springtimes, for it presages the decline of suitable nesting and brood cover.

It is logical to assume that game management technicians might aid grouse by judicious cutting, and perhaps planting—by a precise game of letting sunshine into the swamp. History indicates that this has worked on a grand scale, albeit quite accidentally; it should also pay dividends in penny packets. Suffice to say, it has not.

Imaginative and knowledgeable game biologists have experimented with the selective cutting of pole timber and the introduction of scattered conifers, with the planting of clover at road edges, the burning of second growth, and the calculated development of forest fringes and openings. Technicians have labored mightily—and ruffed grouse have thus far given them a gallinaceous version of the Bronx cheer. Triumphantly, these birds have upset each carefully stacked applecart of logic.

Adjoining acreages of similar ground cover and forest canopy have been studied. In one experiment, biologists attempted to fulfill all the partridge's known requirements by using the chain saw, while a nearby control area was left in its natural state. After several years, a startling discovery was made: the wild, supposedly inhospitable area held more birds than the "improved" land.

Again, where shooting was permitted on one plot and banned on another of equal ground cover and canopy, the termination of a gunning season found more pats on the shot-over hunting ground than in the sanctuary. It would be pleasant to report otherwise, but in no case has habitat manipulation yet resulted in a substantial increase in the number of ruffed grouse on our American continent.

Problems are recognized, but solutions still remain outside immediate possibility because of modern land use and the expense involved in any major undertaking. Certainly the selective cutting of forest canopy to provide the openings that grouse must have in order to rear their broods sounds elementary. Things get sticky only when you realize that low-growing forage plants do not spring out of leaf mold on command, and that ground cover responding to long-deferred sunlight may be far different from that required by immature grouse.

In view of the fact that aspen buds provide a great deal of nourishment for grouse during the winter months, it is logical to assume that *Populus tremuloides* should be encouraged. Similarly, apple trees offer several varieties of food, ranging from buds through foliage to fruits and seeds. Perhaps management could record some advances through the simple planting of apple trees in grouse cover.

Many game biologists now believe that selective and controlled burning is the most promising way to create upland cover. In some areas, notably where conifers are abundant and some native grouse forage exists, the process seems to work. However, one of my favorite grouse hunting areas, ravaged by an early-spring forest fire five years ago, is still a biological desert so far as pats are concerned. Birds are plentiful on the borders of this fifty-acre tract, but they have yet to penetrate. Undoubtedly the future will see resumption of use—but five years is a long time to wait.

Game biologists admit that too little is known about the specific foods that grouse must have in nursery fringes. Some of these must-have plants are obvious, but it is equally certain that it takes time for the right combinations to develop in leaf mold or ashes. Indeed there is a belief that it will be necessary, in re-creating optimum cover, to engage in massive planting and control of shading canopy. Farmers of a lost era did this the hard way by pushing the woodlands back, tilling the soil, and then letting the land revert to its natural state.

To be entirely effective in this highly technical age, successful grouse management may have to be a massive undertaking—and an expensive one. Perhaps a development of forestry practices that will benefit timbermen and hunters alike is one possibility. This is no dream, and it may be realized in the foreseeable future. The knowledge acquired by game biologists in their trysts with failure will be put to good use as natural resources practices mesh for the common good of mankind.

There is time! Fortunately, aside from those mysterious fluctuations of scarcity and abundance, our grouse remains tenacious, fully able to exist with a civilization on the march. Best of all, there are hints that Americans are beginning to check their more than three-hundred-year-old assault upon the life-giving land.

In this fleeting ebb of the twentieth century, we have begun to register concern about the systematic destruction of natural resources. State and federal governments have set aside green-belt areas, to be held in perpetuity for the citizens of the future. Game commissions, in league with sportsmen, have purchased tracts of land that are destined to serve as public hunting grounds for the gunners of tomorrow. Even where these lands are primarily dedicated to the holding of ring-necked pheasants and quail, reared in game farms and released to the gun, wooded sections are sure to support wild grouse. Fortunately, farseeing commissions have set aside territories where pats are already providing grand sport.

Such public lands cannot become housing developments and, like any fringe wilderness, they will attract partridges if the necessary food and cover are there. Until some plausible key to grouse management is discovered, either through new applications or a coordinated approach by timbermen and natural resources agencies, one can rely only on the fact that this great game bird will establish residence in acceptable covers within its general range. There is one exception, and this involves introductory stocking.

As previously mentioned, it is now reasonably well accepted that pats are incapable of sustained flight over any considerable distance. This is why a surprising number of islands, both coastal and inland, lack birds. Game biologists have scored notable successes with island stocking, particularly where live-trapped pats have been utilized. Game-farm biddies seldom take hold in a new environment.

In addition to this resettlement of native stock, there has been much swapping of birds for other wildlife—grouse for caribou, or grouse for a particularly desirable game fish. Assumedly, each party to the various transactions is satisfied. The idea is to barter a well-established species for one that is needed. So long as trading does not involve exotics—which might cause more harm than ultimate good—the practice is wise.

Game biologists generally, but far from unanimously, are now enamored of the idea that "grouse can't be shot out." This, like so many popular clichés, may be extended to rather ridiculous lengths and variously defined.

In any region where pats are reasonably plentiful, it is very doubtful that any cover could be shot out, because the harvested birds would soon be replaced by stock from surrounding woodlands. However, where the population is limited, or even approaching a state of extinction, the demise of any bird might be a tragedy. Certainly natural mortality is many times that of the gun, but—no matter how you slice it—that which you take away is no longer there.

This undoubtedly occurs to biologists who embrace the "can't shoot 'em out" school of thought, for they urge closed seasons on offshore islands where grouse have been introduced. If the initial hypothesis is correct, extended to the ridiculous lengths previously mentioned, then it applies whether there are two pats—or two hundred.

A few game biologists, driving far ahead of this line, are now clamoring for a spring shooting season. They maintain that cockbirds would sustain most of the casualties, since hens are on the nest, and that a harvest of springtime cocks would not adversely affect the species. I hold this morally bankrupt. Regardless of law, I will not kill in springtime.

Bolstering the "can't shoot 'em out" school of thought is a theory of compensation. This holds that "Losses through one agency may automatically protect losses through many other agencies. The death of one individual may mean little more than improving the chances for living of another one." The quote is from Dr. Paul L. Errington's book, *On Predation and Life.*

Probably the good doctor is right, yet there is a possibility that ill-informed game biologists and ardent hunters may draw illogical conclusions, to wit: the more birds destroyed in a given year, the more will be available in a following season. Some qualification seems in order.

One lifetime is hardly enough to see a pendulum swing both ways, but our literature chronicles the market shooter in an era when there were few experienced hunters and no law, followed by a sharp increase in gunning pressure as seasons and bags were decreased. It would seem irresponsible to gamble with extensive lengthening of seasons and undue liberalization of bag limits in an age of massive hunting pressure and declining bird populations caused by modern land use.

Intelligent administration that will administer the renewable harvest so that it corresponds with scarcity or abundance is a high priority requirement, and we can only hope that common sense, rather than any currently popular catch phrase, will guide the actions of game commissioners. We have no moral right to gamble with the future of ruffed grouse.

Generally, game biologists are honest, conservative men, but sometimes they find their jobs threatened by differences with politicians in high administrative offices. Because the ruffed grouse has always been available, because it sneers at artificial habitat and inept management and goes its regal way just beyond the claws of civilization—precisely because this ultimate game bird will not knuckle under to breeders and tamely submit to put-and-take stocking, it may be taken for granted.

Therefore, administrators who are politically motivated, and feel that their positions depend on providing more targets for license holders who can't flush a sufficient number of stocked pheasants and quail, may well decide that the partridge is expendable. It is not pleasant to dwell on the possible exploitation of a great natural resource.

Fortunately, the exploitation of grouse is not an easy accomplishment, for the bird—given adequate cover—resists with remarkable tenacity. As hunting pressures decimate native stock, remaining individuals become hawk-wild. It has been demonstrated that most shooters concentrate on easier targets when these are offered, but turn to pats after seasons on pheasants and quail are closed.

Advocates of longer shooting periods on grouse use this as an argument. Extended pressure will not increase measurably, they say, because the bird is too sagacious to provide an easy target. Moreover, toward the end of a long shooting period pats will be scarce, scattered, and hard to find.

All the more reason to grant them respite, for every grouse brought down by a lackadaisical late-season gunner—who may well be a rabbit, hare, or crow shooter taking a target of opportunity—will be one less to survive the grinding attrition of wintertime and be on hand to drum in April.

Cynical biologists declare that, law or no law, the late-season shooter will clobber grouse. I am optimist enough to believe that poaching is committed by a small minority and that an overwhelming majority of outdoorsmen hew to the letter of the law. Sportsmen have been blamed for many things, but it is not the dedicated hunter of partridges who promotes longer seasons and heavier kills. Those of us who love the bird prefer a safe harvest.

To a great extent, the future of ruffed grouse hunting will depend upon an improvement in human manners. Many of my favorite covers are now plastered with signs promising instant mayhem if anyone dares to trespass. Thus the owners and I, together with a select group of friends, are permitted to enjoy some of the best of partridge shooting.

A small number of so-called sportsmen must take all responsibility for this sorry state of affairs. There are precisely three reasons why landowners place their acres off-limits to transient gunners, and only one of these is morally questionable.

There is the individual who purchases a sprawling hunk of real estate and posts it to ensure that he and his friends will have a private hunting ground. The fact that no game is stocked, and that the acreage is neither improved nor managed means nothing to these latter-day land barons. They take possession and henceforth monopolize native game that should be available to all citizens. Though the practice burgeons with each succeeding year, it remains a minor problem. But what of tomorrow?

Property rights are inviolate, and I am too fond of American democracy to suggest any socialization of upland coverts. Nonetheless, some latter-day Solomon among jurists or legislators might profitably devise ways and means to prevent personal exploitation of a natural resource by landowners who reap, but never sow, a harvest that traditionally belongs to all free men.

This in no way should be considered an indictment of those who manage game preserves where other birds and mammals are regularly stocked, managed, and harvested cleanly by those who pay for the privilege, or by the owner and his guests.

There exists today, and probably always will be with us, a minority of landowners who quite honestly believe that hunting is a mortal sin, who desire to see no living creature killed, and who believe that by posting land they provide sanctuary for harried birds and beasts of the woodlands. I cannot agree, but neither will I argue the point. Indeed I hold the true believer in high esteem: at the very least he is honest.

My operations on posted territory are confined to acreages that are forbidden to transients because the landowners have had quite enough of knuckleheads who lack good manners and common sense. Ignorant gunners who blast away at pheasants on country lawns or within a few yards of the housewife's window work a great disservice upon careful, mannerly shooters.

Of course it is axiomatic that the average grouse hunter will blame all indiscretions on those who gun for pheasants. Ringnecks are barn-yard fowls: they delight in foraging through truck gardens, fields of standing corn, and assorted produce. Stupid shooters thus find every opportunity to make themselves persona non grata. On the other hand, neither the grouse nor the pheasant hunter is absolved of all blame because of his choice in game birds.

One of my favorite sidehills is owned by a schoolteacher who is reputed to be an enemy of all sportsmen. When I plan to gun that area, I call and ask permission to hunt—and always I receive a cordial invitation to come ahead. This landowner simply wants to know who is combing his back forty. He is allergic to strangers and he will call the police whenever an interloper appears. That's because some cretin once slaughtered two of his cats (on the front lawn) and another drove a charge of bird shot through his kitchen window.

Another rimming and ancient woodlot is owned by a dairyman who has had his cows peppered by sadistic hoodlums masquerading as sportsmen. His land is tightly posted, yet he has invited me to hunt grouse. One July afternoon, after I had helped him find a cow that had dropped a calf far down in the bottomlands close to a big swamp, the dairyman allowed that he'd let my friends hunt that country during the coming fall. "But tell them to ask permission first, and to use your name as a reference."

"Permission to hunt" is a key phrase, and it will become more important as we move into the future. Landowners generally raise no fever over hunters, but they flush to apoplectic levels when vandals leave gates open, cut or break fences, shoot livestock, and blast small shot at the geraniums in kitchen windows. Who would quarrel?

End of a perfect day for a country gunner.

This state of affairs probably began with the industrial revolution that set up two diametrically opposed societies. Suddenly the city worker began to regard husbandmen as inferiors. The fact that a farmer might have studied Greek and the calculus at some major university was ignored: he lived in the boondocks, hence he was a savage whose knuckles dragged on the ground when he walked erect. Posting began after the first ignorant interlopers began to treat countrymen as subhumans. When fences were smashed, orchards raided, and gates left open the landowner rebelled. He posted KEEP OUT signs and, where necessary, he defended his property with buckshot or rock salt.

Still, 90 percent of the posted lands in these United States can be hunted by those who ask permission and who appear to be responsible, intelligent citizens. The average farmer is likely to be a shooter himself: he has no complexes about guns or a fair harvest, and he never envies the bag of a visitor. If his land is ringed with signs, you can bet he has his reasons.

Most of us now employ motor vehicles to travel from covert to covert, and there is always a temptation to pull into any farm lane and park. If the landowner happens to need this access, he will be understandably irked by the roadblock. It is no more than common courtesy to leave a car where it will not impede working traffic.

Cordial farmer-sportsman relations are far more important than the average shooter realizes: they are based on the fact that gunning in American coverts is a privilege, granted by landowners; it is not a right, and those who engage in the sport must learn that they are guests, subject to certain disciplines and gentlemanly conduct. Initial contact with men of the soil often cements relationships and launches friendships that last a lifetime. This is an honest act between men who are equally concerned with the land and the wildlife that flourishes upon it.

Primarily, the partridge hunter is a northern man. However, every American shooter dreams about an encounter with this greatest of game birds, and the future will see much greater emphasis on grouse. More leisure time, greater affluence, and rapid transportation guarantee the ascendancy of the sport. Finally, there is a psychological involvement, an evolutionary thing common to every enthusiastic outdoorsman.

First, whether gunner or angler, he seeks the easiest and surest meat on the table. Next, he begins to specialize and to utilize fishing tackle and firearms that require skill and finesse in their employment. At the end of it, if a trophy trout raised to a fly becomes the only fish worthy of mention, and a well-antlered buck the only possible reward of a big-game hunting expedition, then a ruffed grouse halted in midflight with a charge of 8's is the ultimate thrill in upland shooting.

In America we grope toward the rewards of high skill in rod and gun sport, not to the slaughter of fish and game. Gradually, those new out-doorsmen who haunt the "chicken farms" where pheasants are re-leased the night before their befuddled flush into a hostile sky will grow weary of a sure thing and seek the challenge of this wildest of the wild.

North American sportsmen need grouse, if only because this is one of the few great native game birds still abundant on our continent. Quail are tremendously important, and pheasants certainly are the choice of a multitude—but bobwhite and the hardy ringneck can be raised in game farms at a cost entirely agreeable to the advocates of put-and-take. The partridge cannot.

Yet, if they are guarded and cherished, ruffed grouse will be avail-able long after urban sprawl and the No Trespassing signs of em-battled farmers have placed pheasants and quail off limits to all but the cruisers of public hunting grounds and preserves. Grouse will be in the river bottoms, on the birch slopes, and in the fringe conifers of a mil-lion rugged acres across the smiling face of this land.

They were first to greet the Pilgrims, and they'll be the last to endure when the cement and steel arteries of progress push most of our guns into metropolitan museums.

But you and I, our children and our children's children, will be long gone when that happens. Indeed the partridge may survive us all, for he steps around adversity, cocks a wary, glittering eye at mankind, and takes possession of whatever fringe wilderness remains on the flower-ing earth of the American northland.

SELECTED BIBLIOGRAPHY

ASKINS, CHARLES. *Game Bird Shooting*, The Macmillan Company, 1931.

BENNETT, LOGAN J. *Training Grouse and Woodcock Dogs*, G. P. Putnam's Sons, 1948.

BETTEN, H. L. *Upland Game Shooting*, Penn Publishing Co., 1940.

BUMP, GARDINER, ROBERT W. DARROW, FRANK C. EDMINSTER, and WALTER F. CRISSEY. *The Ruffed Grouse*, New York State Conservation Department, 1947.

CHAMBERS, ROBERT E., and WARD M. SHARP. *Movement and Dispersal Within a Population of Ruffed Grouse*, Journal of Wildlife Management, 1958.

CRISSEY, WALTER F. *See* BUMP, GARDINER.

CROSS, GORHAM L. *Partridge Shortenin'*, Privately printed in a limited edition of one hundred copies, 1949.

DARROW, ROBERT W. *See* BUMP, GARDINER.

EDMINSTER, FRANK C. *The Ruffed Grouse*, The Macmillan Company, 1947.
———. *See also* BUMP, GARDINER.

FORESTER, FRANK. *Frank Forester on Upland Shooting*. Edited by A. R. Beverley-Giddings, William Morrow & Co., 1951.

FOSTER, WILLIAM H. *New England Grouse Shooting*, Charles Scribner's Sons, 1942.

KNIGHT, JOHN ALDEN. *The Ruffed Grouse*, Alfred A. Knopf Co., 1947.

LEOPOLD, ALDO. *Game Management*, Charles Scribner's Sons, 1939.

MADSON, JOHN. *Ruffed Grouse*, Winchester Press, 1969.

PALMER, WALTER L. *Ruffed Grouse Flight Capability over Water*, Journal of Wildlife Management, 1962.

SCHEMNITZ, SANFORD W. *Fall and Winter Feeding Activities and Behavior of Ruffed Grouse in Maine*, Wildlife Society, 1970.

SHARP, WARD C. *See* CHAMBERS, ROBERT E.

SILVER, HELENETTE. *History of New Hampshire Game and Furbearers*, New Hampshire Fish & Game Department, 1957.

SPILLER, BURTON L. *Grouse Feathers*, The Derrydale Press, 1935; The Macmillan Company, 1947.
———. *Drummer in the Woods*, D. Van Nostrand Co., Inc., 1962.

TAPPLY, H. G. *The Sportsman's Notebook*, Holt, Rinehart & Winston, 1961.

(Italics indicate photographs)